All That Internet Crap

Learn to Use the Web to Build Your Business and Achieve Your Dreams

MCS Mahone

All That Internet Crap
Learn to Use the Web to Build Your Business and Achieve Your Dreams

MCS Mahone

True Anomaly LLC
8351 Ronda Dr
Canton, MI 48187

Disclaimer

While considerable effort has been made to ensure the accuracy of the information herein, this book is intended for teaching beginner entrepreneurs and may contain simplifications or other technical inaccuracies. If you feel any of the content is incorrect and would like to suggest a revision, or if you find typos or other errors, you may submit them to contact@trueanomaly.com. Pease include the book title, page number, and error details in your email.

Entrepreneurship is risky and may result in loss of capital or other penalties. Neither the publisher nor the author assume any liability for errors, omissions, or damages resulting from the use of the information contained in this book. Code snippets contained in this book are provided with no warranty expressed or implied. Use of information, code and links provided in this text is at your own risk. Products and services mentioned in this book are for informational purposes only and their mention does not constitute an endorsement of these products or services.

No part of this book should be taken as legal advice. This book does not replace legal advice. A qualified attorney should be consulted prior to all business activities.

Legal Issues

Table of Contents

Preface

My first attempt at a startup was a flop. I had just finished college and launched an online clothing brand with some friends, but I had no idea how to design and build a website, optimize it for search engines, or how to use social media from a business perspective. Sales were low, and we eventually spent more money than we made. Determined to find out what we had done wrong, I read dozens of books—eventually becoming a complete web developer. After that, other friends and acquaintances began asking me for advice on their own entrepreneurial objectives, and I found myself answering the same questions over and over. I realized there were an awful lot of entrepreneurs searching for the same information, so I decided to write this book to make it easy for entrepreneurs to learn this information in an efficient way, and help them avoid a costly startup disaster.

Purpose

This book aims to get you up-to-speed on the modern skills needed to be a successful entrepreneur in the shortest time possible. This book acts as a single resource, replacing the need to buy dozens of books on different IT topics. The average entrepreneur need not spend months or years mastering HTML, CSS, DNS, email, and other things just to build a custom website with a domain name. Why buy dozens of books only to read a few pages out of each of them?

The goals of this book are as follows:

1. Teach the basics of the Internet and web
2. Provide sufficient background knowledge required to setup an online presence for a business
3. Teach business skills applicable to online businesses
4. Provide context for online tools that grow and sustain a business

This book will not teach you how to use any specific domain registrar, website builder (CMS), or in-depth web development. Instead, you will learn how domains, websites, email, search engines, social media and other tools work, so that you can use any services' tools with confidence.

Chapter 1 will define some of the basic terms of the Internet that will be required knowledge for the chapters that follow.

Chapter 2 will focus specifically on how websites are built, defining the technologies underneath them, and showing how to use this knowledge to better use a CMS. Chapter 3 will focus on setting up email for a domain and the services that providers offer. Chapter 4 will look at search engine optimization techniques to assist your site's appearance on search engine listings. Chapter 5 will provide tips and best practices for social media usage. Chapter 6 is an entrepreneurship chapter aimed at optimizing the graphic design and usability of your website.

Finally, Chapter 7 focuses on using analytics to monitor your site traffic, and other tools that make your workflow easier. The Appendix provides some additional important information that all online entrepreneurs should know.

Who This Book Is For

This book is for entrepreneurs with no technical background looking to get a basic, top-level overview of the information technology skills required to run a successful small business in today's high-tech world.

What This Book Does Not Cover

Of course, opinions differ on what are "essential skills" for an entrepreneur. This book does not cover Ethernet, VPNs, Wi-Fi, Operating System troubleshooting, virus protection or removal, server administration, or programming. I consider these essential skills for IT professionals, not necessarily entrepreneurs, although this book will certainly serve as a prerequisite if you should decide to expand your knowledge to include these topics.

Prerequisites

I assume you have used a computer, sent some email, and feel comfortable with web browsers, and smartphones. No programming experience or knowledge of computer science is required.

Companion Content

Almost all of the content in this book is — or will be — discussed in video form on the MCS Mahone YouTube channel https://www.youtube.com/channel/UC3-MYnHYaYIqZejdiQRorJA/.

Errata may be found at https://trueanomaly.com, and code contained in the book at the GitHub page https://github.com/trueanomaly/intforbusiness.

Contact Us

If you have questions about the material, reach out to me using @mcsmahone on Facebook, Twitter, or Instagram.

If errors or technical inaccuracies are found herein, please contact us at contact@trueanomaly.com. Please include in the message the page number and quotation of the error.

Please address all other inquires to:

True Anomaly LLC
8351 Ronda Dr
Canton, MI 48187

Ready? Let's Go!

The first two chapters of this book are the most difficult. They introduce an awful lot of topics in a hurry, such that you may finish them feeling a bit dizzy. That's okay! These chapters introduce a whole bunch of things that will be mentioned in later chapters, but complete understanding is not necessary. Keep moving forward, and the topics will clear up in time.

Okay, as a business owner, I'm sure you have better things to do than read this book, so let's quit wasting time and get going!

CHAPTER 1
Internet Basics

So you want to build a business with an online presence? No problem. The steps required are as follows:

- Buy a domain name
- Build a website using a CMS
- Point your domain to your website
- Start selling

The specific steps to complete the above can be found in help documentation on the websites of the service providers. This book aims to provide some context to the documentation so that you can follow the instructions with confidence, and optimize your site for sales. We are going to learn what the Internet is (from a technical perspective), what websites are, the protocols they depend on, what domains are, and how DNS records and cookies work. These are probably terms you have heard, but now we are going to define them and get a sense of how they function.

The following section will throw a lot at you at once. The nature of the Internet requires learning a few topics all at the same time. Each will be explained here, so don't worry if terminology comes up that you don't understand. Stick with it.

The Internet is a network of computers connected by wires or wirelessly. These computers are further divided into two main groups: **servers** and **clients**. If you are reading this book, you have likely only used a client computer directly. Your desktop, laptop and smartphone are all clients. Clients connect to the Internet and receive an **IP address**, and then make **requests** to servers for files or data. Servers issue **responses**. Clients contain software called web browsers that handle all of the gritty details of making requests to servers and translating their responses into something friendlier for humans to read. Figure 1-1 illustrates these terms.

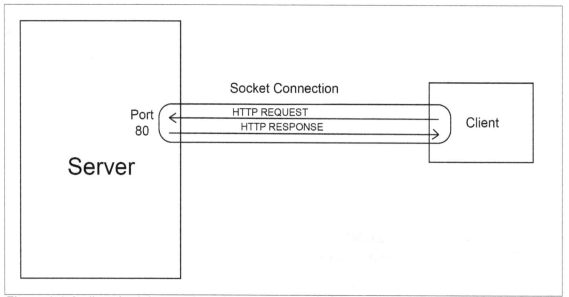

Figure 1-1 A client (web browser) getting a web page from a remote server using an HTTP request sent through a socket connection. The server receives such requests on a port. Reprinted with permission, Learning to Build Apps (2018 True Anomaly LLC).

The World Wide Web is built on top of the protocols that define the computer network known as the Internet. Computer data is just zeros and ones, and a computer can only tell what data goes where if the data is structured in a very specific way. Just like procedures in human life require following protocol, computers accomplish this by following protocols, except computer protocols are much more strict. No deviation is allowed or the communication may fail. Fortunately, computers are very good at doing the same task over and over.

One of these protocols is called the **Internet Protocol**, and all computers "connected to the Internet" are given an IP address. For clients, this IP address can change depending on where and when they connect. For servers, this address remains the same so that clients can send them requests at the same place, much like businesses prefer to keep the same address so that clients can reach them. Unlike clients, servers also tend to stay in one place and remain powered on and ready to receive requests.

Figure 1-2 shows the protocol stack that makes all the technologies of the Internet and web possible. You can think of the Internet as the Internet Protocol (IP) and the **Transmission Control Protocol** (TCP), as these two protocols form the basis of computer-to-computer communication. They ensure data sent from one computer arrives at the right destination and in the right order. Many familiar technologies are built on these two protocols, and they in turn operate according to their own protocols. The web, for example, uses HTTP, which we will define later. Together, these protocols form a protocol stack.

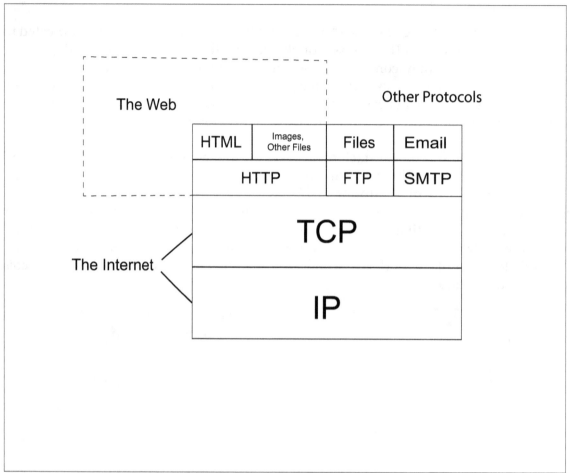

Figure 1-2 The protocols of the Internet, the web and related technologies. You won't have to know how these protocols work; just know they work together to ensure that data sent between clients and servers arrives completely and in the proper order.

You are probably familiar with the concept of files in a folder on a computer. You may not have known that each file on a computer has a **file path**, which tells the computer (or human user) where to locate that file on the hard drive. This file path can be written as a **URL** (Uniform Resource Locator). Each file on a computer hard drive has a URL. You can use a web browser to view files on your computer by typing in the URL of the file, which starts with file:// and then the local file path. **Local** refers to things on your computer hard drive, as opposed to **remote**, which refers to files on another computer hard drive. Remote files are files in a folder stored on another computer. If that folder is hosted by a web server, then you can access those files with a web browser by typing in the URL, staring with http://.

Figure 1-3 shows opening a PDF file on the computer using a web browser. You can see in the address bar the URL of the file (which is just the location, or **file path** on the computer). You can see the URL starts with file://. This tells the browser to locate the file locally.

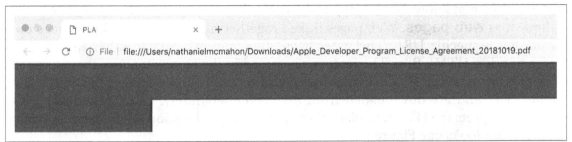

*Figure 1-3 Using a web browser to access a file on the hard drive. After the file:// protocol identifier the local file path relative to the root directory (/) and the file name complete the URL in the browser address bar. Notice the third forward slash (**file:///**) representing the root directory. See the appendix for more on this.*

When you pull up a website on a web browser you are really just accessing a file on a remote server rather than your own computer. You do this is by starting the URL with http:// rather than file://. This tells the browser that what comes next is the address (domain) of the computer on which to find the file. Everything after the address is the relative file path (that is the location of the file relative to the website folder on the remote server).

Don't worry, people cannot just download files from your personal computer by typing in http:// followed by your computer IP address and file path. This is because an HTTP request for the file goes to a port on your computer, and that port will not be open unless you have server software on your computer that opens it.

This concept of accessing remote files with a web browser leads to the concept of web pages and websites.

Websites

Websites are a folder of files stored on a remote server. A web browser downloads a special file known as the **index file** when it first accesses a domain. This index file is written in a format known as the **Hyper Text Markup Language** (HTML). HTML files are known as **web pages**. Web pages linked together form a **website**. Every page on a website has a specific URL. The index.html* file contains links to other files such as images or other HTML files. The images are stored in the same directory that stores the index page, or possibly inside a subfolder (subdirectory). These images have their own unique URLs and are downloaded from the server separately. Once downloaded, the browser interprets the HTML to place them in the proper location on the page. A typical website folder looks like Figure 1-4.

Figure 1-4 The directory structure of a typical website includes subfolders for images, helper functions and library code (classes), CSS and JavaScript (discussed in Chapter 2).

There is one file called the index file (shown here as index.html) that is in the **web root** folder. Other folders include css, and images. These folders hold other files. Every file in the web root folder or its subfolders has a distinct URL.

---

*If the website is database driven (defined in Chapter 2), the index file extension may be the language of the server side program that grabs the data such as PHP, ASP, JSP or something else. In these cases the index page is index.php, index.asp, index.jsp, or something else.

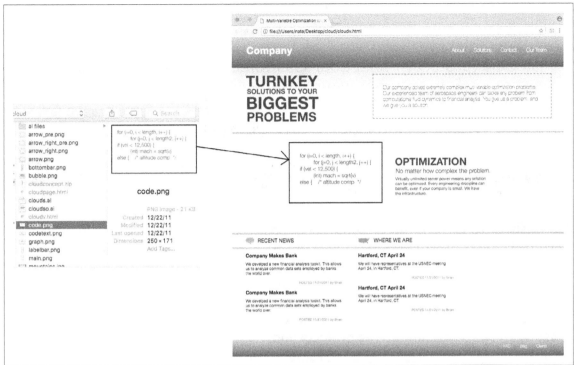

Figure 1-5 How a web browser builds a website from files in a folder stored on a remote server. The HTML contains an img tag with a src attribute containing the URL of the file which the browser can understand, then download from the server. Reprinted with permission, Learning to Build Apps, (2018 True Anomaly LLC).

Figure 1-5 shows a web page being rendered in a web browser. The files in the folder on the left are used to create the rendering on the right. When you type in example.com to the address bar of a web browser, the browser is actually requesting the index file from the server even though you didn't type in example.com/index.html.

To review, every file on a computer has a URL. Local URLs are called filed paths. Remote URLs are files on a different computer. Remote URLs of HTML files on a web server are called web pages. Let's now look at URLs a little more in depth.

Uniform Resource Locators

Remember, URLs are more general way of writing file paths. Unlike file paths, they are not restricted to files on a local machine, or even to a particular protocol. Let's look at the format of a URL to discuss these elements in more detail. Figure 1-6 shows the elements of a URL.

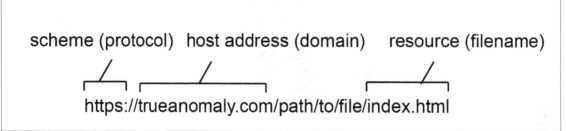

Figure 1-6 A URL format; in parenthesis are some terms loosely equivalent to help you keep track of all this new terminology. URLs are sometimes called URIs. Reprinted with permission, Learning to Build Apps, (True Anomaly LLC 2018).

Although http:// is the common protocol when accessing websites, other protocols exist. The file:// protocol can be used to access files on your own computer with a web browser, as we saw earlier. You may have also uploaded files to a server using FTP at some point. This operation uses the ftp:// protocol, even if you weren't aware of it.

Now that we have identified the structure of a URL, let's talk briefly about two of its constituent elements, namely, the protocol and domain.

HTTP

The HTML files, image files, and any other data sent between the server and the web browser are packaged in a protocol known as the **Hyper Text Transfer Protocol** (HTTP). HTTP, and other protocols it is built upon, act as envelopes for content sent between servers and clients. You won't have to know anything about HTTP. Just know that a web browser acts as an agent that takes care of the technical details of crafting requests to servers and interpreting the server responses, and a stack of protocols (IP/TCP/HTTP) ensure the data is received completely and in the right order. HTTP is the standard format with which clients can request files from remote servers, and also the standard format in which servers package their responses. Figure 1-7 shows a browser translating a URL into an HTTP request. You type in an address (domain) and the browser handles the complex details of crafting the formal request according to the protocol.

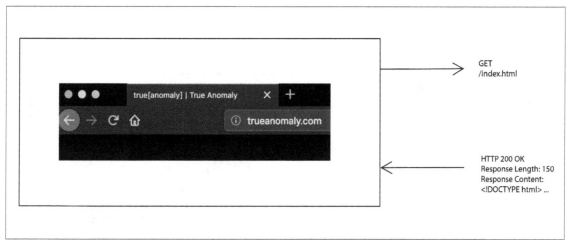

GET
/index.html

HTTP 200 OK
Response Length: 150
Response Content:
<!DOCTYPE html> ...

Figure 1-7 A browser acting as a user-agent, crafting HTTP requests from a URL in the address bar.

A web browser takes a URL and crafts an HTTP request, then processes the HTTP response it gets from the web server. All of this happens behind the scenes, and the purpose of this discussion was just to explain why http:// appears in the address bar of the browser.

HTTPS and SSL Certificates

You may have noticed when accessing most websites that https:// appears in the address bar instead of http://. The "s" means that the connection is secured using **transport layer security** (TLS) because the website owner has obtained an **SSL certificate** for the server. Secure connections are designed to protect users from man-in-the-middle or wire sniffing attacks, where a hacker in between the server and client listens to the connection to steal usernames, email addresses, passwords, credit card information, or other sensitive information.

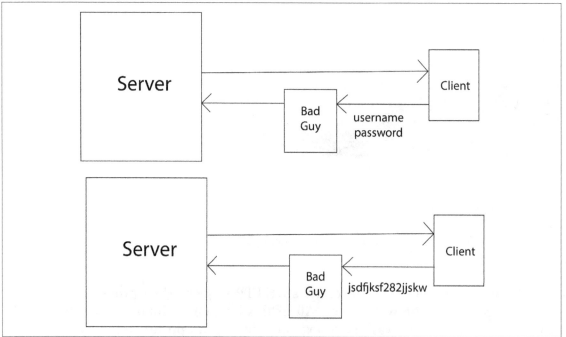

Figure 1-8 A man-in-the-middle can intercept and read content sent between a server and client unless that content is encrypted in a way that only the server and client can interpret. The top image shows an attacker intercepting a username and password in plain text whereas the bottom image shows an attacker intercepting the content but getting nothing usable since it is encrypted using TLS. The encryption shown here is not accurate; it is for demonstration only.

Figure 1-8 shows an example of such an attack. A man-in-the-middle can intercept requests and present the user with a fake website pretending to be the site they requested, or they can simply listen in on the connection to steal data from it.

TLS works by encrypting the connection with mathematical cryptography methods, so only the sender and receiver know the message. This process is known as completing a **handshake** between the server and client, which is like an agreement between the two parties as to how to encrypt the message. This means that if someone successfully intercepts the connection, they get an encrypted message, which is like stealing a safe without the combination. The handshake process is more complex than you need to know, but if you're interested, check out this link:

IBM
(https://www.ibm.com/support/knowledgecenter/en/SSFKSJ_7.1.0/com.ibm.mq.doc/sy10 660_.htm)

Secure connections are absolutely critical when sending or receiving email addresses, usernames, passwords, and credit card or banking information. Secure connections slow the process of serving the page down a bit, which is why some websites are served initially as plain http://, but the connection is upgraded to https:// before presenting the user a form requesting secure data (such as a shopping cart checkout). Many websites prefer to secure every connection even when sending and receiving less critical data or viewing less critical pages. This also can enhance user confidence in your website (see Chapter 6).

SSL certificates are purchased from certificate authorities like Thawte (https://www.thawte.com/), although because the process of configuring a server with a certificate is a bit technical, most website service providers (like Shopify, or Squarespace) include this in their fees and do the setup for you. When your server is setup properly, the browser address bar should display https:// and a lock symbol that is locked.

If there are issues with the setup, the browser usually displays an unlocked lock and may display a warning page. This indicates a problem with the TLS connection. Warnings can also be generated from **mixed content,** which occurs when the page itself is served securely but includes content (images, stylesheets, or scripts) from insecure connections. Mixed content is just as risky as an insecure web page, just as a locked safe with a hole in it is not much better than no safe at all. We will talk more about how mixed content can occur in Chapter 2. Check out this link for more.

Google (https://developers.google.com/web/fundamentals/security/prevent-mixed-content/what-is-mixed-content)

Domains

Domains are a short term for **domain names**, which are like phone book listings. Domains are names that can be translated by a **Domain Name System** server into an IP address.

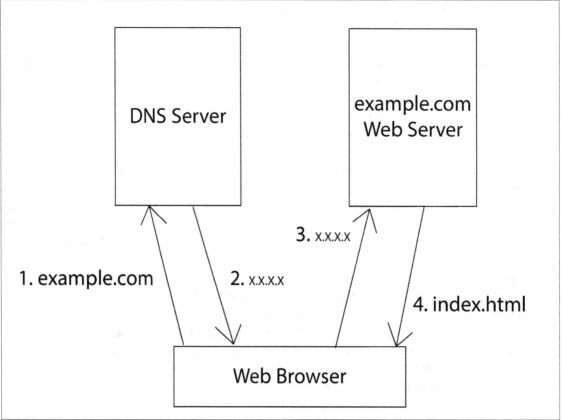

Figure 1-9 The process your browser goes through to get the IP address corresponding to a specific domain. Steps 1 and 3 are HTTP requests just like we discussed already. The addresses are represented here as "X"s but an IP address is actually four numbers separated by periods.

If you open a browser and type in example.com into the address bar, the browser sends a request to a DNS server to find the A record associated with example.com. The server returns the IP address of example.com's server, and your browser then sends a second request to that IP address for the web page. Check out Figure 1-9.

The request to the DNS server to get the IP address happens so quickly and transparently that most users don't even realize it happens. Browsers can also **cache** this information, which means they store it for later reference for a specified time period. After the specified time period, the cache is refreshed (the browser requests the information again to ensure it has the most up-to-date information).

If you happen to know the IP address of the server you are trying to reach, you could type that into the browser address bar instead of the domain name and it would still get you to the proper server, bypassing the DNS address lookup step (steps 1 and 2 in Figure 1-9).

Buying a domain is also known as registering a domain. A domain registrar charges some money—likely annually—to reserve the name and put the information you specify into the **WHOIS** record. This record contains all the registrations of all domains on the web.

When you own a domain, you also own any **subdomains** of your domain. For example, if you own example.com, you also own go.example.com or blog.example.com or anything else you want to put in front of your domain. Your domain is actually a subdomain of the higher level domain "com", which is actually a subdomain of the top most level domain "." (although the dot after com is usually omitted from addresses). Since virtually all subdomains of "com" have been taken, they have added many other extensions (like "co" for example) to increase the space available. Some of these new subdomains have not been fully implemented yet, so "com" subdomains remain the most commonly known and are thus the most sought after, but as people get familiar with the newer extensions that may change. Picking a dot com domain is the safest from the standpoint of user familiarity and backwards capability of technology, as old web code may not validate the new extensions. For example, when registering for an account on a website, the code on that site may not let you register with an email address of a domain extension it does not recognize.

When searching for a good domain name you may find that some are extremely expensive. The price of a domain is usually based on how relevant, short, and snappy it sounds. Some people buy good domains just to sit on them and hope to sell them for a profit someday. You may want to read Chapter 4 on search engine optimization before you purchase a domain name, as it has relevance in this area.

Some common domain registrars:

- **GoDaddy** (https://www.godaddy.com/)
- **Google** (https://domains.google.com/)

Also note that some website builder services (like Shopify or Squarespace) may offer domain registration and hosting as well. See Chapter 2 for more details on such services.

DNS Records

When you buy a domain, you are really buying access to the DNS records of that domain, also known as a **zone file**, which can be modified by the domain control panel. Figure 1-10 shows the records stored on a DNS server (a.k.a name servers). Why are there so many records? Your domain registrar does not have to be the same company that hosts your website! Nor does the company you use for email services have to be the same as the company that hosts your website! If you use different companies for these different services then those services will be on different servers with different IP addresses. We illustrate this later on.

To review, in Figure 1-9 we saw the process your browser uses to find the IP address from a record stored on a DNS server. Access to this record is what you are buying when you purchase a domain.

The DNS records contain a number of entries, each coded by letters, along with a value for that entry, typically a numeric IP address or domain name. The **A records** tell which server is hosting the web page associated with that domain. This is the record your web browser accesses when looking for the server that hosts a web page. When you purchase a domain and build a site on Squarespace or Shopify or another website builder, you will point your domain to Squarespace or Shopify's servers by putting the IP address(es) of their servers in the A record of the zone file of your domain. You may also see AAAA records. These refer to the same thing as A records, but map to an **IPv6** (think version six of the Internet) formatted IP address. IPv6 is not fully adopted yet, so don't worry about that right now.

The second record we will look at is called **CNAME** for canonical name. This record is used to specify another equivalent name for the domain, and the value of this record tells the domain of the server to locate if this equivalent name is requested. The most common use case is to redirect calls to www.example.com over to example.com (notice the lack of www). It was common in the early days of the Internet to preface all web page domains with www (world wide web) but this usage has become less common, and most hosting providers include these records for backwards compatibility. You may notice some websites redirect the root domain to the www subdomain, but this is typically done with a serverside redirect rather than with DNS (i.e. you need a developer or CMS setting to do that).

The third record we will look at is called **MX**. This record specifies the domain of the server that hosts email for this domain. In Chapter 3 we will discuss why setting this record properly will help ensure your email does not end up in your customer's spam folder.

Another record you may come across is **TXT**. These records typically contain a small token value usually used to verify domain ownership. An example is Google Analytics, which may ask the site owner to verify their domain ownership by placing a very specific TXT value in their DNS records. Analytics are discussed in Chapter 7.

TTL is an acronym for Time To Live, and it simply tells clients how long to believe the record before checking again. You put a TTL on each record; the default is one hour, which you can safely leave alone.

You can also lock or unlock the domain. Unlocking it allows it to be transferred to another registrar. You only need do this if you decide to change registrars, say from GoDaddy to Google, for example. Normally, your domain will remain locked.

@	A ▾	1H	IPv4 address	+	ADD

Name ❔	Type ❔	TTL ❔	Data ❔		
@	A	10m	192.30.252.153	DELETE	EDIT
@	TXT	2m	"i=164&m=domains-mx2-p8"	DELETE	EDIT
www	CNAME	1h	trueanomaly.com.	DELETE	EDIT

Figure 1-10 A sample set of DNS records in Google Domains.

Figure 1-10 shows a screenshot of DNS records. These records are not private information; they are in fact hosted on a publically accessible server (which is what you want, as if they weren't no one could find your domain). Access to edit these records is private, and you should protect your domain registrar login credentials. There are such things as private domain servers for reselling domains or use within large companies, but they are not our focus here.

In the figure, @ refers to the root domain (the name you bought), and the other records in the name column are subdomains of the root domain. For example, the ftp record refers to ftp.example.com, where example.com is the root domain. Each subdomain can have a complete set of records (CNAME, MX, etc.) that are different from the root domain. This means that subdomains can utilize different providers for these services (web host, email host, etc.) than the root domain. What you enter in the data column (the value of the record) depends on the type of the record. A records take an IP address as the value, CNAME records take a domain name.

Domain forwarding is a service provided by a domain registrar that allows you to forward all requests to your domain to another domain. This is useful when you want common misspellings of your domain to simply forward to the proper domain, or to prevent competitors from buying similar sounding domains and forwarding them to their site. Sometimes people purchase multiple versions of their domain name with .com, .biz, and .net extensions, or common misspellings of their domain, to prevent this kind of activity.

The domain registrar you use and DNS host do not have to be the same company. If that confuses you, just register a domain and don't change anything! The company that hosts your DNS file provides the addresses of their name servers (the IP addresses of their DNS servers). The company you registered the domain with will set them to their own servers by default. You only need change them if you decide to use two different companies (one as the registrar, one as the host). Even if you transfer your domain to new registrar, the new registrar should set these for you. You will only need to change them manually if you want to, so if you don't want to, don't mess with them! If this is still confusing, take a look at Figure I-II.

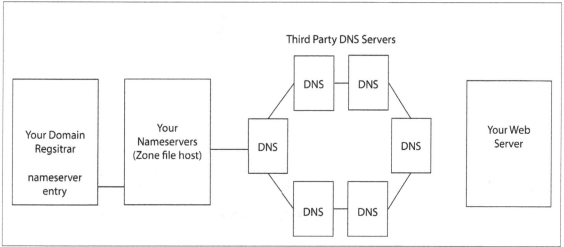

Figure 1-11 Your domain registrar, zone file host, the DNS system, and your web host, are all different players, although some companies offer multiple services for customer convenience. For example, your domain registrar hosts your zone file by default unless you manually change the nameserver entry. Also some web hosting providers also provide domain registration and zone file hosting. Other services like email can be provided by still other providers on other servers.

DNSSEC is an optional setting that aims to protect your domain from some attacks that attempt to spoof and redirect users to a different domain posing as your domain by corrupting the cache (stored DNS records) in DNS servers. You can think of it as a way to let your web browser do a double check that the record (IP address) it is receiving from the DNS server is correct. If your registrar makes it easy to do, you can turn it on if you want to. It is usually default to leave it off, because of very technical issues it can cause. You may not have these issues, but some people leave this setting off anyway, with the idea that the risk is low enough.

Remember, different subdomains of your domain can point to different servers. Figure 1-12 shows a sample DNS entry if we wanted to make blog.example.com point to our **Tumblr** (https://www.tumblr.com/) blog. We are setting the value of the record for blog.example.com to the name of the domain of Tumblr's servers (which we get by reading their developer documentation). If we kept this record in place, when someone accessed blog.example.com in the browser, their browser would display that in the address bar, but behind the scenes would be sending the request to Tumblr's servers. Note, some configuration is required on the Tumblr account as well, so that their servers know where to direct the request when a user requests it. See their help documentation for more information.

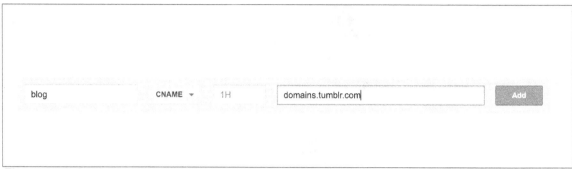

Figure 1-12 Setting a record to direct users of our blog (blog.example.com) to our Tumblr page in Google Domains. The domain for Tumblr may change, check their documentation for the latest information.
(https://tumblr.zendesk.com/hc/en-us/articles/231256548-Custom-domains)

If we wanted to add a TXT record (required by some services to verify domain ownership) we would keep the first field as @, change the record type to TXT, and fill the last field with the value the service provider gives us. Their servers will then ping our DNS records and see if the value is correct, thus proving that we do indeed have access to the domain's records.

For more information, check out this link:

Google Support (https://support.google.com/domains/answer/3251147)

Cookies

Cookies are small pieces of data put on a client by a web server that allow the server to identify the client. Cookies are then sent to the server on every request, allowing the server to identify the client. This allows users to login to websites, and stay logged in until they logout. They can also be used to track users as they move around the Internet, a feature commonly employed by advertising firms. Cookies are why you may see ads for websites you just visited on another site. Cookies can be cleared in web browser preferences, although this will log you out of most websites. Whenever possible, it is always a good idea to stay logged out of websites until you need to be logged in. This is like keeping your seat belt fastened on an airplane in cruise flight (not always required, but always a good idea). This is because many attacks by hackers are designed to take advantage of users who are logged into websites already (this is far easier than trying to guess passwords).

So how do cookies track us around the web? Websites often contain code and content from other sites, for example, ads are often served from third party ad servers. Code from third party sites can also place cookies on your browser. In fact, every time you request a web page your browser may receive cookies from any server that has embedded code on that page. Code embedded on the site can read cookies of the same domain that the code came from. This means that code that serves ads on one site can read cookies that the same third party server placed there when the browser visits a different site. It may seem a bit convoluted, but it works. Code from third party ad servers is all over the web, and that code places cookies on your browser unless you specifically disallow this in your browser settings.

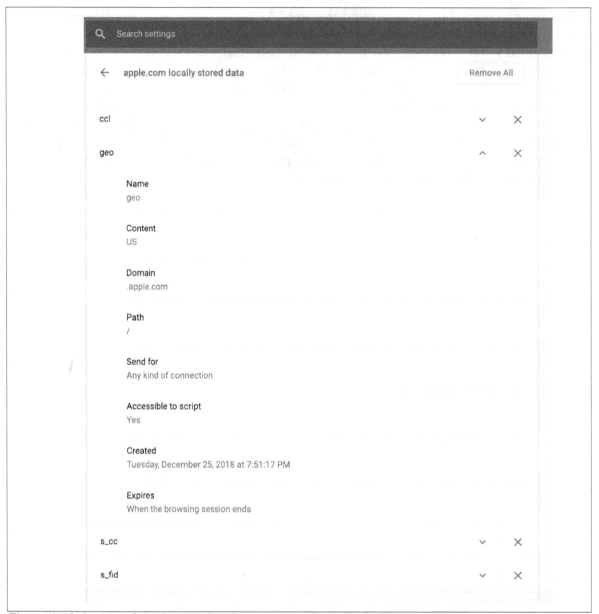

Figure 1-13 A view of the keys and values along with some additional metadata about one of the cookies stored in our browser. You can see these in Chrome by going to Preferences->Advanced->Content Settings->Cookies->See all cookies and site data.

Cookies are not code. They are just plain text keys with values such as name=nate. Figure 1-13 shows viewing cookies in Chrome. This cookie has a key of "geo" and a value of "US".

Review

Whew! That was a lot. In this chapter we learned that the Internet is composed of computers connected together, specifically servers and clients. Each computer gets an IP address. Clients send requests to servers, which issue responses. The requests and responses are packaged by a stack of protocols that ensure all data sent between clients and servers arrives properly, and in the correct order. At the top of this protocol stack is HTTP. Secure connections occur using HTTPS, which works the same but uses an encrypted connection.

Websites are folders of individual files, including graphics files, images and web page files. Web pages are files that are written in HTML, which is the code that makes up a web page. Every file in the folder of a website has a distinct URL. This URL can be typed into a web browser address bar to download the file. The web browser handles all of the crafting and interpreting of HTTP, as well as parsing and displaying HTML. Below that computer operating systems, modems and other network hardware handle the TCP/IP connections and data transfer.

URLs contain the IP address of the computer we wish to access, but this is more commonly swapped out with a domain name, because of the ease of remembering names. The servers that translate domain names into IP addresses are called DNS servers and work a lot like address books. Purchasing a domain name gives us access to the DNS records, which indicate the IP addresses of the servers that host the website, email, ftp, and any web services of other subdomains. By changing the records in the zone file, we can utilize different companies (different servers) for our domain registrar, web host, email host, nameserver host (zone file host), blog host, or any other services we desire.

Chapter 2
HTML, CSS and Templates

Chapter 1 has some great information, but none of it really allows you to build a great looking site and get sales! Now we are going to look at HTML and CSS which combine to create the templates on which a great business website is built.

We mentioned in Chapter 1 that a website is a folder of files stored on a remote server. We talked about how a web browser first requests the index file, which contains links to other files that instruct the browser how to render the page. This index file is in a format known as HTML. HTML is the basic computer language of web pages. It contains content and **tags**, which tell a computer how to display the content. Writing content this way is known as marking up the content, and it is thereafter called **markup**. Because HTML is the language of web pages, writing it is a great skill for digital entrepreneurs to have. Let's start by looking at HTML a little more in depth.

Note: you should install as many browsers as your operating system supports (such as Firefox, Internet Explorer, Chrome, Safari). Each of these browsers render CSS a bit differently, and as you have no way of knowing what browser a particular customer is using, it is important to know what your customers see. You can get them all for free by downloading them, but not all are compatible with all operating systems, and some have different versions for different operating systems. If you don't have both a Windows machine and a Mac, borrow a friend's computer to test your site on it. The more computers, operating systems, tablets and smartphones you test, the more you can ensure the homogeneity of your client's browsing experience. Some links are provided below:

- **Google Chrome** (https://www.google.com/chrome)
- **Mozilla Firefox** (https://www.mozilla.org/en-US/firefox/new/)

Web Page Source Code

To see the code that makes up a web page, open a web page in your browser and right click and select "View Page Source". The exact process varies based on what browser you have: do a web search for "viewing page source in [your browser]" if you can't find it.

This will open a new page that displays the actual HTML content of the page. You will see that some of it is readable, and some of it looks like gibberish. You are looking at a combination of two things, the content (the part you can read) and **tags** (for computers to read). Once you learn HTML, you will know what the tags mean too, but for now just realize that the tags are for the browser to interpret. The difference between the rendered web page and the source code is that the browser has removed the tags around the content and styled it with any linked CSS style sheets. Figure 2-1 shows the source code of a web page and the rendered web page. Let's talk more about the tags.

Figure 2-1 The source code of a web page (top) and the rendered page in a web browser (bottom). Open a browser and try viewing the source for yourself to get a better view.

HTML Tags

As mentioned in Chapter 1, **HTML** stands for Hyper Text Markup Language. A **markup language** is a language of **tags** (one opening, one closing) that wrap the content. These tags are computer readable because they follow an exact pattern using less than, greater than and slash symbols. This pattern can be recognized by a computer and that allows us to program instructions that tell the computer how to display, style, or manipulate the content. Each tag follows the general pattern shown below:

<tag>This is content.</tag>

Example:
<h1>This is a top level header.</h1>

These tags are interpreted by the web browser in a process called **parsing**. Once the HTML is parsed, the tags are stripped out of it before the content is displayed. HTML is a language consisting of many tags, each with a one letter or one word identifier that indicates what kind of tag it is. **P** tags are for paragraphs, **div** tags indicate natural divisions in the content that are essential for layouts, **h1, h2**, etc. tags are for a hierarchy of headers. If you have ever taken a technical report writing course you are probably familiar with top level headers and sub level headers and their styling.

You don't have to read a whole book on HTML to get comfortable with a few of the most common tags. In addition to the ones mentioned, other common tags are <**span**>, to wrap single elements, <**script**>, to link JavaScript code, <**link**>, to link CSS code, and <**a**>, to link to other web pages. Tags can be nested, in which case the wrapper is known as the **parent** tag, and any tags within it are known as **child** tags, such as below:

<div>
    <p>This is a paragraph nested in a page division. The paragraph is a child of the div
    tag. The div tag is the parent tag of this paragraph.</p>
</div>

HTML Attributes

In addition to tags, HTML contains **attributes**. These are actually part of the tags themselves. Attributes give additional information about the tags, such as the ID of the tag, its class, its purpose, and other things. With attributes, we can show a more complete view of a general HTML tag:

<tag attribute="attribute_value">Content.</tag>

Example:
<h1 id="header1" class="home-headers">This is a top level header.</h1>

This example shows a top-level header with an ID of header1 and class of home-headers. If we assign IDs and classes to tags, we can target them to style the content with another language called CSS. Any tag can have as many classes as you want, but only one ID. An example of a tag with multiple classes is shown below. The classes are separated by spaces.

<p id="sample-para" class="xtra-margin biggerFont coolParagraph">Hello.</p>

CSS

CSS stands for **Cascading Style Sheets**. Style sheets are files that include instructions for a web browser to display the HTML content. They follow the following format:

Selector {
  Property: value;
}

Example:

#header1 {
  color: red;
}

The **selector** is a string of HTML tags, classes or ids that select which parts of the document to apply the styles specified inside the brackets. In the example the selector selects a tag with an ID of header1, and sets its text color to red. The pound sign (or hashtag) is the CSS symbol for ID. Remember attributes in the last section? Attributes like IDs and classes allow us to target a specific tag (in the case of an ID) or a group of

27

tags (in the case of a class). In this example we targeted one particular header tag. But we could also target a group of header tags, such as all the header tags on the home page, for example. In this case, we give each header tag on the home page a class of home-headers (you can actually name them anything you want, and include dashes or numbers as necessary) in the HTML (as a class attribute). Then, in the CSS, we would write:

```
.home-headers {
  color: red;
}
```

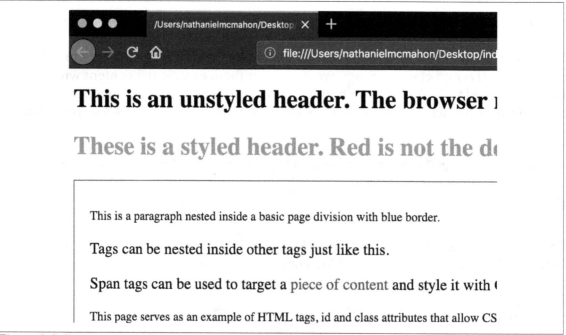

Figure 2-2 A screenshot of some of the code available on the book GitHub page. This shows HTML content similar to that described in this chapter being styled in a number of ways by targeting tag id and class attributes. Go to the book website to access the code and download the index.html and style.css files to open in your own web browser.

The period before home-headers is the CSS symbol for class. Classes are used to target groups of content, IDs are used to target on a single piece of markup (a single tag).

Which style takes precedence is the most specific style, that is, the one that uses the most selectors or the most specific selector. CSS gets very advanced and there are ways to target just about anything, for example, the first child element of h1 tags with a class of home-headers.

The simplest way to include styles in HTML is to code them inside a <style> tag right in the HTML somewhere. The more common way is to put them in a separate file and include that file in a <link> tag.

More than one style sheet can style an HTML document (web page). In fact, it is common to have many style sheets styling the same page, all included by their own individual <link> tags in the <head> section of the HTML document. So if multiple styles from the same or other style sheets are targeting the same tags, how do we determine which styles take precedence if those styles conflict?

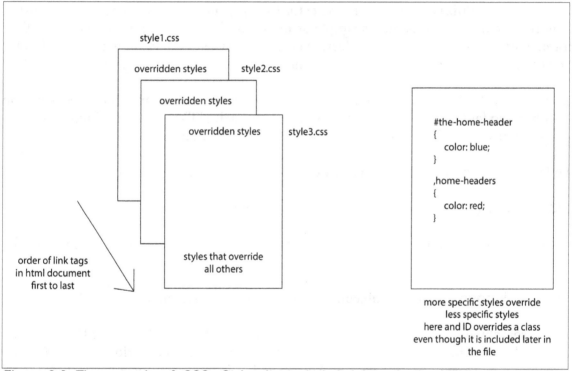

Figure 2-3 The cascade of CSS. Style sheets included later in the HTML document take precedence over styles linked before. Also, styles that occur later in the same style sheet override styles that occur before. However, as shown in the right of this figure, more specific styles, regardless of where they are included, override less specific styles. Targeting ID attributes is more specific than targeting classes.

Figure 2-3 shows the cascading nature of style sheets, where the last one included in the HTML takes precedence over the ones before it, just as styles applied later in the same style sheet override the rules that are applied first. In addition, the styles cascade in the sense that styles applied with more specific selectors take precedence over general styles.

The purpose and advantage of the cascade may not be obvious at first. It becomes clearer when you build a large website and see how much CSS code there is. Thousands of lines of largely duplicated code will make clear the need for classes over IDs, as well as the need to override some of the styles (but not all) of a particular class for an individual element. Remember, the cascade is only about determining precedence when styles are applied to the same element. Elements are the HTML tags and content targeted by a CSS selector.

CSS cascade and precedence seem very straightforward but get rather complex when working with design frameworks and other people's code, as anything you want to override must utilize a more specific selector to apply the style properly. Often choosing a more specific selector is not as simple as targeting the tag based on its ID. Often CSS frameworks utilize very specific selectors (such as first list item child with class of bold-box of unordered lists with a class of blue-list). Whew! That's a very specific selection!

Don't worry if this was overwhelming. If you want to learn just one thing, focus on the CSS box model to learn how your browser treats each HTML element. Memorize this: margin, border, padding, content. To tweak position, use margin.

To learn more about CSS, buy a book dedicated to it or check out the following link:

W3 Schools (https://www.w3schools.com/css/default.asp)

Also check out the book code shown in Figure 2-2. This will demonstrate some of the basics:

This book code (https://github.com/trueanomaly/intforbusiness)

When searching for a book on CSS, you may see some books referencing CSS 3, which will likely focus just on the features of version 3 of CSS and are written for those who already know version 2.1 and below. Your best bet is to search for a basic HTML/CSS introductory book and learn both languages together, as they are in many ways linked. The same goes for books about HTML 5; they will likely be specific and assume you already know HTML. However, any introductory HTML/CSS book can and should be updated to reflect the changes of HTML 5 and CSS 3, because it is not necessary that you learn the newer versions of each language separately.

An HTML / CSS Web Page

Although all web pages have different content, markup, and styles, the overall layout of an HTML document is always the same: it is a bunch of tags nested inside the <html> and <body> tags. It is shown in Figure 2-4. The content inside the <body> tags is what changes from page to page. There is no content in the example in Figure 2-4, but a typical web page would have dozens or hundreds of <div> tags nested inside the <body> tag.

```
<!DOCTYPE html>
<html>
 <head>
  <title></title>
  <link />
 </head>
 <body>
  <script></script>
 </body>
</html>
```

Figure 2-4 The layout of an HTML page never changes. Styles are linked in the head of the document. Scripts may be included anywhere in the document but often just before the body closing tag for better page loading performance. Only the content in divs, paragraphs, and other tags in between the body tags changes from page to page. The page content, if we were going to add some, would go after the opening body tag, but before the opening script tag.

Note that the <head> tag is for HTML information. This is different from the header of a web page (which is typically a <div> tag inside the body). The header of the web page is usually a navigation bar (navbar) that includes the company logo and links to other pages on the site. As of HTML version 5, there are specific tags for the navigational header and footer.

We also need to talk about the <img /> tag, as it is very important for web developers. Images are arguably the most important part of a business website, so understanding the image tag is important. It is one of the rare tags that has no closing tag. It contains a **src** attribute, whose value is the relative URL of the image that is supposed to be displayed. It also has an **alt** attribute that is the text that should be displayed in the case the image does not load, or if the page is being viewed by a screen reader. An example is shown below:

<img src="images/logo.png" alt="Example Company Logo" />

Creating an HTML / CSS Layout

Creating a web page layout with HTML and CSS is complex, too complex for this book, particularly when we want that layout to look good on all screen sizes and devices (a topic known as **Responsive Web Design**). To at least give you an idea of how layout in CSS works, check out Figure 2-5. In the figure you see how a page layout is divided into divisions (<div> tags) and those div tags are placed in different positions on the page. Placing the divisions in their proper place is done with a combination of CSS styles including position, float, margin, width, height, and others. This is shown in Figure 2-5.

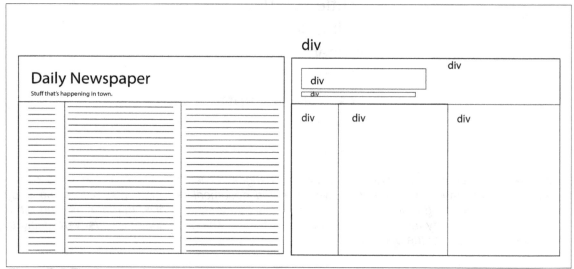

Figure 2-5 The layout of a newspaper on the left with the equivalent HTML layout on the right. Each column, header and content is wrapped in a page division (div tag). A layout is created by floating divisions to position them in the desired places.

Web pages are composed of dozens or even hundreds of individual nested divisions. Some divisions are to place content in the right spot on the page. Others provide a target to apply a specific style via CSS and make that content look different from other content on the page.

Because of the difficulty in creating layouts with explicit CSS code on differing screen sizes, entire books focus on CSS for responsive design, which usually include the use of a responsive grid, which is premade CSS written to provide a framework for placing content in places on different screen sizes. The idea of a responsive grid is simple: divs can sit next to each other on larger screens and stack on smaller screens. Figure 2-6 shows how the divisions in Figure 2-5 stack vertically on a smaller screen width. Responsive grids are possible because of lines of CSS known as **media queries**, which allow you to specifiy different styles to the same content depending on the screen size.

In practice, it's complicated. If you're feeling ambitious, do a web search for responsive design and grids and dive into the learning. By the time you finish you may end up in a different career!

To review: HTML documents are plain text files consisting of nested tags and their content. The most common tag is the <div> tag (i.e. division tag) that divides the page into sections. Divisions are used to create layouts, as well as provide targets for CSS styling. By "targets" we mean that the tags provide something for CSS to use as a

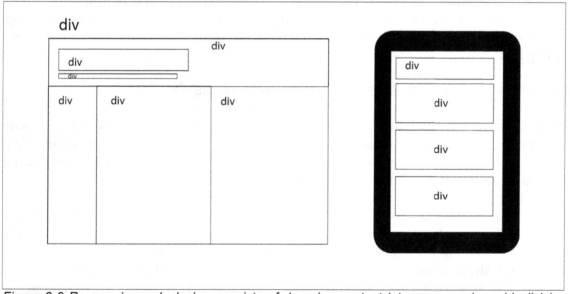

Figure 2-6 Responsive web design consists of dropping content into a responsive grid: divisions with widths set by CSS media queries. This allows divisions to sit side-by-side in wide layouts (left), and stack on smaller screens like phones and tablets (right). This behaviour is not default to HTML and must be programmed by the responsive grid.

selector: namely, the tag itself, or an ID or class attribute. Why is this so complicated? Computers can't be told, "grab the third paragraph in the News column and color the text blue." Instead, computers can recognize patterns of characters (tags and their attributes). As long as these tags and attributes follow the exact syntax everytime, the computer can recognize them and use the CSS selector to know which areas to style. You give div tags a class and/or id attribute to differentiate them from the other div tags. Now take a look back at some web page source code and see if it makes anymore sense.

How a Browser Builds a Page

So now that we have seen both HTML and CSS in action, let's learn how to link them. CSS styles can be hard coded into HTML inside a <style> tag, but due to length, stylesheets are typically separate files included in HTML with a <link> tag. The order the <link> tags appear in the HTML file determines the order of precedence of the styles within them.

Figure 2-7 shows the process of a browser building an HTML web page. It first requests the index page from the server. After parsing the response, it sees that it needs a CSS file, a logo image, and a JavaScript file so it requests those using the value of their respective href and src attributes. If there were multiple CSS or JS files, they would also be requested. The exact order in which these responses are received is unknown, but it doesn't matter, as the CSS cascade is determined by the order in which the <link> tags appear in the document. An example of a link tag is shown below, note there is no closing tag:

```
<link rel="stylesheet" type="text/css" href="bundle2.css" />
```

The URL in the href attribute is relative to the path that served the HTML, which is why it doesn't contain a domain name or protocol or anything else. If the stylesheet were in a different folder (a subfolder of the web root folder) that would be shown here with the folder name followed by a forward slash and the file name.

The index.html file may contain references to files on other servers. This is common when JavaScript or CSS frameworks are used. So the connection in Figure 2-7 actually looks more like Figure 2-8, with different connections to different servers occurring simultaneously. In Chapter 1 we talked about mixed content in the HTTPS section. You can see now how such a thing would happen, as content that makes up a web page is loaded from many different files, even files on different servers.

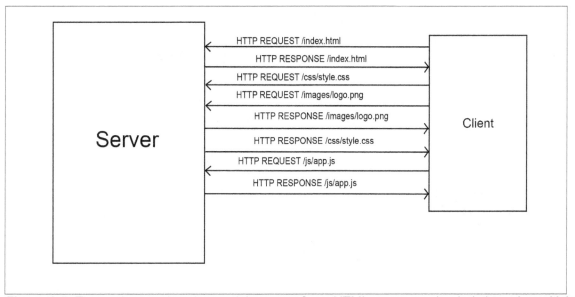

Figure 2-7 The scripts and styles and images of an HTML page are loaded through multiple requests, often utilizing one or more socket connections. Sometimes these requests actually go to separate servers that host the files (see Figure 2-8 next). Style.css and app.js are common names but style sheets and JavaScript code can have any file names. Reprinted with permission, Learning to Build Apps, (2018 True Anomaly, LLC).

Don't worry, the task of making sure all content is loaded over secure connections falls on the theme developer (discussed later), so you only need to check their work, and ensure changes you make or href and src attributes you add are correct. We will discuss this more later. Using relative URLs for files on your web server, or specifying https:// in the URLs for files on third party servers will ensure that no connections are insecure.

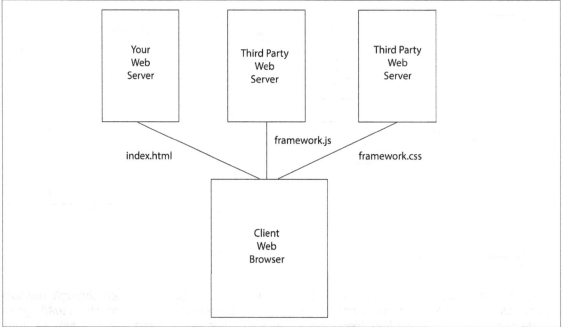

Figure 2-8 Often images, JavaScript and CSS frameworks are loaded from third party servers known as Content Delivery Networks. This takes some of the load off of the server that hosts the index page.

Web Developer Tools

Although made for web developers, web browsers come with tools that can be useful for website owners to view how the code is styling the HTML on their website. To open them on Chrome choose View->Developer->Developer Tools. On Firefox, Tools->Web Developer->Inspector. On Safari, Develop->Show Web Inspector. You can also do a web search to find how to enable them if these instructions don't match your browser version.

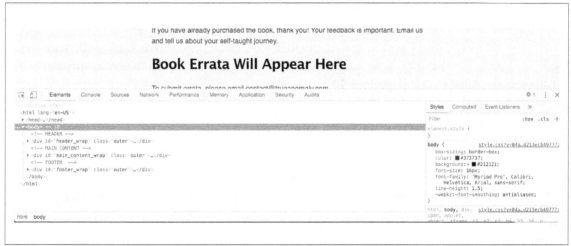

Figure 2-9 The web browser developer tools in Chrome. The HTML source of the page is on the left under the Elements tab, with the CSS styles applied to the highlighted section visible on the right. Scroll down in the right sidebar to see the box model for the highlighted element.

You can even tweak the code and view the changes in real-time, but this does *not* change the code, it just allows you to preview your changes. To actually change the code, you need to locate the appropriate file in your CMS (discussed next) and edit it and save it. Figure 2-9 shows the browser developer tools open, showing the page HTML on the left and the CSS styles of an element on the right. Clicking on the CSS property you want to change will highlight it and allow you to play with it.

You can see how HTML/CSS combine to make a beautiful web page. Unfortunately, they don't do much actively. HTML can link to other pages, and CSS has some ability to create some simple animations or change properties on mouse position, but these languages do not have the ability to send or receive data to or from a server. That means that static HTML pages cannot do much other than display content. All interaction with the server causes requires loading a new page. Now we're going to talk about how to make those static sites more dynamic, by including programming code in a language known as JavaScript.

JavaScript

JavaScript is the programming language of the web. It is what allows websites to work like apps on a computer or smartphone. When you click buttons, JavaScript code is what does the work behind the scenes. When a modal window (discussed later) pops up when you first go to a site, and then you click the "x" in the corner and it goes away, JavaScript code is what makes all that work. For most businesses selling products or displaying services, JavaScript only functions to create widgets and enhance the design and usability of the site. JavaScript may also be used to send data to a server by your shopping cart/checkout process, and/or payment gateway (see Appendix) integration. As a business owner, unless you want to build a business that utilizes an app, you won't need to learn JavaScript. You can leave the programming to web developers. An example code snippet is in Figure 2-10.

```
<script type="text/javascript">
document.getElementById("header1").onclick = function() {
 document.getElementById("header1").innerHTML = "hello world";
};
</script>
```

Figure 2-10 The small snippet of JavaScript code inside an HTML script tag. It may look confusing, but JavaScript is the code that powers all web applications. Like CSS, it can target HTML tags and content. Here we find an HTML tag with an ID attribute of header1 and set its content to "hello world."

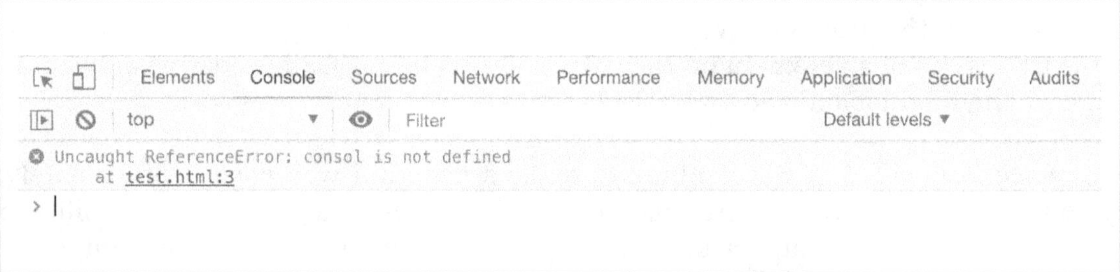

Figure 2-11 The JavaScript console displaying an error. If any of the JavaScript code on a web page fails to run, due to a syntax or other error, it will display in this console.

The web developer tools mentioned previously also include a console for viewing JavaScript errors on your site. Although you won't be writing the JavaScript code, they can allow you to check the quality of the code you are using. Some errors can safely be ignored as they won't affect your site's functionality, but ideally your site should have no JavaScript errors and the developer console will be empty. Figure 2-11 shows a JavaScript error in the console. If you see something like this, contact the theme developer. Theme developers are explained in the next section.

Databases

You may have used a database directly, but if not, you have almost certainly used one indirectly. If you have an account on virtually any website, your data is stored in a database. Many common databases use **SQL** (structured query language) to store the data in tables, and retrieve it with programmatic queries. A sample SQL type database table is shown in Figure 2-12.

User ID	Username	Email	Password	Blocked	Last Login
1	dude68	dude@trueanomaly.com	ksalk2984iusf	0	7284783739
2	jane273xl	jane@trueanomaly.com	lkaskf89s72k9c	0	7337478393
3	Kay282xkw	kay@trueanomaly.com	98asiofkccik	0	8363849944

Figure 2-12 The sample table full of data in a fictional database. Reprinted with permission, Learning to Build Apps, (2018 True Anomaly).

Now let's see how databases power database driven websites.

Content Management Systems

The previous discussion of HTML included the content typed in between the tags. This is known as **hard coding**, because in order to change the content, the user would have to open the file in a text editor and change it. This is undesirable because non-technical people do not want to get too deep into code and risk deleting something important. Because most business owners do not want to design and build their own websites, several companies build **Content Management Systems** (CMS) that allow non-technical users to customize a website by means of a graphical user interface. These are web-based JavaScript programs which allow a user to set their text content into a database, upload custom photos into image place holders, and customize things like text, colors, and which components appear in which locations without creating or changing code.

With a CMS, the content is not hard coded into the HTML. Rather, a variable is placed inside the appropriate HTML tag or attribute, or CSS property. This variable is replaced by database content when the page is requested from the server by a customer's web browser. When variables are placed inside HTML, the files are known as **templates**. This shown in Figure 2-13.

You may not see the term CMS used as much anymore by the paid services. Most companies that offer this today simply call them "online builders" or "interactive website tool" or something. Whatever they call it, they are all web based JavaScript programs that allow non-technical users to create and change online content without writing code. Many also allow the user to change themes and even edit the HTML/CSS code as desired.

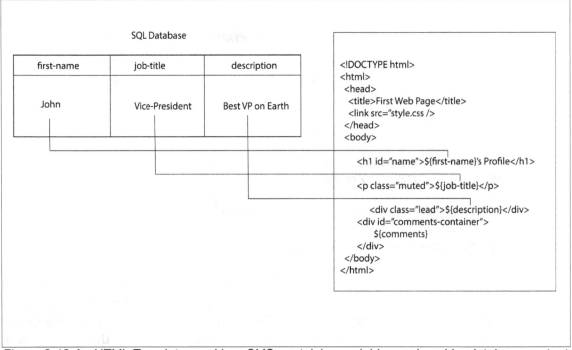

Figure 2-13 An HTML Template used in a CMS containing variables replaced by database content. The format (syntax) of the variables depends on the templating language used, some use brackets or dollar signs.

Themes are a group of HTML templates, CSS and JavaScript that contain variables that are populated with the user content. Professional web designers who build these are often called **theme designers**.

HTML/CSS templates are the heart of themes. The CMS allows the user to change the value of different CSS properties such as font size, text color and other things. Depending on what the theme offers, the user may also add or remove **widgets**, also known as **components**, such as datepickers, product selectors, search boxes, and other things.

The web pages of a CMS website do not exist as distinct HTML files as described in Chapter 1. Instead, when a client requests them, the CMS uses code to build the page by populating HTML templates with database content stored by the website owner. This is the process shown in Figure 2-13. This means that the URLs of a CMS website are not individual HTML pages but rather the terms in between the forward slashes are instructions that tell the server which page to build. The URL requested is basically a command for the server, telling a program on the server which page to build and return to the client. This architecture is known as a **database driven website**.

As a quick aside in Chapter 1, we mentioned that database driven sites have their index files end in .php or .asp or something else. Some URLs may not end in a file at all! This depends on the configuration of the server, but either way, the URL of database driven sites does not necessarily correspond to a specific file, but rather triggers code to run on the server to build a file. The HTML of the page doesn't even exist until the server code builds it from a template file!

Due to the nature of web languages (HTML, CSS, JavaScript), it occasionally is necessary to inject some logic into these templates. For example, sometimes you may want to style every other item in a list a different color. In these cases a simple variable placeholder will not do. That is why themes rely on a templating language, which is like a mini programming language that allows designers to make changes to the way things are rendered without having to get deep inside the code that actually powers the website. Shopify uses the Liquid **templating language**. Learning a templating language is only necessary if you find that a premade theme is inadequate for your needs.

Liquid (https://shopify.github.io/liquid/)

Here are some examples of content management systems (a.k.a. website builders).

Some are tailored specifically for online storefronts, where others specialize in general websites for small businesses:

- **Squarespace** (https://www.squarespace.com/)
- **Shopify** (https://www.shopify.com/)
- **Wix** (https://www.wix.com/)
- **Square** (https://squareup.com/online-store)

Open Source CMS Alternatives

For the true DIY pro, there are free, open source CMSs available. Before online website builders were the norm, web development companies would setup one of these for their clients to allow their clients to administer their own website. You will still need to buy a domain, SSL certificate, and pay monthly for hosting. **Shared hosting**, where your website is hosted by the same server as other websites, is enough for most small businesses. Many domain registrars also offer shared hosting services. Implementing one of these takes web development skills that go beyond what this book covers, but if they seem appealing check out the following:

- **Joomla** (https://www.joomla.org)
- **Drupal** (https://www.drupal.org)
- **Wordpress** (https://wordpress.com)

You will need to setup a server and will likely want to acquire at least a working knowledge of a serverside programming language such as PHP. If you are not particularly savvy at managing servers, you will definitely want to choose a hosting service that offers **cPanel**, **phpMyAdmin**, and the option to provision your server with your SSL certificate automatically. If becoming a developer is not your cup of tea, stick with the paid CMS services mentioned previously.

The advantage these solutions offer is virtually unlimited flexibility, complete control over themes, and modular additions of functionality, at the cost of significant complexity and learning curve. The ability to add modular functionality is a significant benefit however, particularly for those who desire their site to function like a web application, with social networking, customer reviews, and other features.

Building a Website with a CMS

Regardless of which CMS you choose, to build a business website with a CMS you must:

- Design a logo
- Take pictures of your products/services
- Pick a theme
- Populate your theme with your own content
- Point your domain to your CMS

In order to layout your site with templates, it helps to understand a little of how they work. Templates are made for pages and components. Many templating languages allow templates to be embedded inside other templates. Page templates can be specific to a specific page, such as the home page template, or generic, meaning the About Us, Contact, and FAQ pages might share the same generic template. In addition to page templates, there are also templates for components. Component templates get embedded inside the page templates. You will only need to modify HTML/CSS of the templates if certain aspects of the theme do not work for your use case. As long as you are careful not to mess with the variables inside the templates, you won't break any functionality, but you may make your site look ugly! Document your changes so you can reverse any bad results.

Many CMS's use one URL for an administrator (or backend) web app, on a domain they choose (usually a subdomain of their domain), that allows the site owner to enter the database content, and another URL (your domain name) that allows customers to see the customer facing site. Both sites access the same database content. This is shown in Figure 2-14.

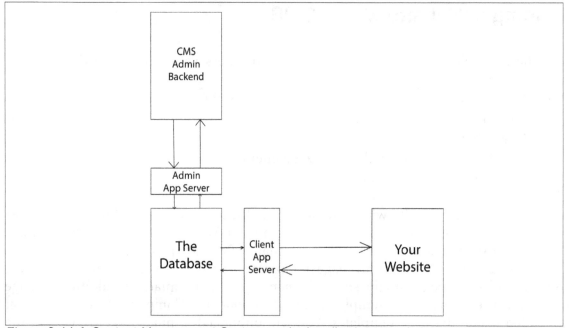

Figure 2-14 A Content Management System works by allowing an administrator to enter data and settings into a database through an admin backend. The same database data is accessed by the client app. This setup utilizes two different domains for admin versus client. Some content management systems utilize the same app servers and have both the admin backend and customer facing site on the same domain, with the different views controlled by user permissions. Not shown here: images and graphics you upload may be stored on the app server or a CDN, with their URL stored in your database.

Figure 2-14 shows how the administrator (that's you!) accesses the database through a different site than the one shown to your customers. Both sites access the same database, the admin site sets the content and settings, the customer site simply retrieves it.

Even though the actual architecture behind the scenes is quite complex, involving a database server, one or more app servers, and possibly a CDN, do not get overwhelmed. For all intensive purposes your website is still just a folder of files (HTML templates, images and graphics files) along with your content in a database.

User Interface / User Experience Design

You have likely used, but may not know the names, of common user interface components such as modals, carousels, scrollspys. You won't be building these components yourself (unless you want to be a web designer), but by learning the terminology you will be better equipped to understand the features of themes and communicate with theme makers or web designers if you choose to hire some.

Modal windows are the pop-up windows that you probably either love or hate. Unlike the pop-ups of the 90's and 2000's, these do not open a new browser window but rather cover the background in a dark tint that goes away and hides the modal if the user clicks anywhere but the modal window itself. These are commonly triggered when a customer first accesses the website to encourage sales with some sort of promotion for entering their email, for example.

One web design that is in vogue is the parallax. Images best suited for a parallax design are those with space (or depth), such as landscapes with a clear fore, middle and background. This makes the user feel as though they are looking out to something. Check out Chapter 6 for more information.

For more examples of common web components, check out:
Bootstrap (https://getbootstrap.com/docs/4.1/components/alerts/)

Although components may seem different, they are still built out of HTML/CSS/JavaScript, just like the websites they live on. Figure 2-15 shows some examples of common user interface components.

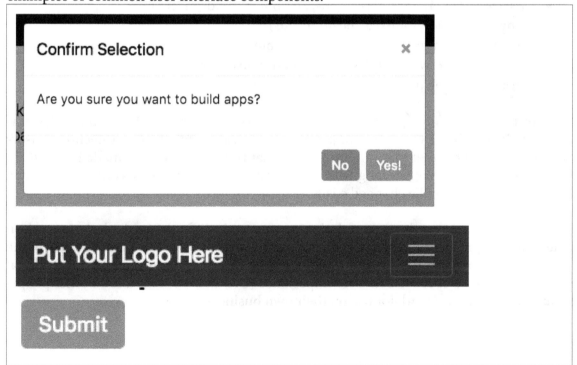

Figure 2-15 Modals, navbars, and buttons are all common UI elements. The button in the navbar is known as the "hamburger" button and it is commonly used on navbars intended for display on smaller screens. Reprinted with permission, Learning to Build Apps, (2018 True Anomaly LLC).

Review

In this chapter we learned about HTML and CSS, and how the two languages are used to build web pages. The first page requested by a web browser when accessing a domain is the index page although this file is not displayed in the browser address bar. The index file contains links to other web pages on the site, or to other sites, as well as links to images that are displayed on the page. The CSS file(s) instruct the browser how to layout the page, what fonts and colors to use, how much space to put between elements on the page, and more.

The essential topics of HTML are:

- Tags (div, a, link, span, h1, h2, etc.)
- Attributes (id, class, href, src, etc.)

The essential topics of CSS are:

- Selectors (HTML tags, classes, ids, attributes, children, etc.)
- Properties (color, font-size, position, etc.)
- Box model (margin, border, padding, content)
- Cascade order (which styles apply when styles overlap)
- Responsive web design

In order to make coding up a website easy for everyone, Content Management Systems were developed. These web apps are JavaScript programs that allow non-technical users to upload custom content to a database server that is used to fill in premade HTML/CSS templates. These templates, along with some JavaScript components, combine to form a CMS theme, which can be changed easily.

Finally, we learned that the task of designing themes is difficult, particularly in modern times with the proliferation of smart devices and a myriad of screen sizes. Because of the difficulty of responsive web design (RWD), theme design is often done by professional web designers who specialize in User Experience (UX) design. This allows other people to purchase their hard work for use on their own business website.

Chapter 3
Email

You have probably used email before. Running a business with email from a custom domain requires just a bit more knowledge to get it all setup and configured, but then it works just the same as your private email account. Let's begin by looking at the types of email a business can send to clients.

Email Types

There are three types of email messages a business can send to clients:

- Transactional
- Newsletter
- Marketing

Transactional messages are any type of message associated with a customer action on your website or brick and mortar business. Order confirmations, shipping notifications, billing errors, order delays, account email or password changes, and more, are examples of transactional emails. These types of emails are typically allowed by email provider terms and conditions.

Newsletter emails are opt-in subscription emails that keep your customers informed about news and products or services of your business. They are sent to each address on a mailing list. Professional mailing list services such as Constant Contact and MailChimp can be helpful, as they provide templates for HTML emails and also have built-in unsubscribe functionality. Crafting good looking HTML emails is very difficult unless you are an expert in HTML and CSS. Also, managing subscriptions and unsubscribe actions from mailing lists manually is not a very productive way of doing business. Allowing clients to unsubscribe is required by most mailing list service providers' terms and also may be required by law in some jurisdictions. When sending a mailing list email manually, do not use **carbon copy** (CC), as all CC address are visible to all recipients, and exposing other people's email addresses is a privacy violation and may result in legal action.

Marketing emails are any type of unsolicited advertisement email not part of a subscription mailing list. These emails are commonly known as spam, and mailing list service terms specifically limit or outright prohibit their usage. While sending spam mail is extremely common, it is important to know that it is not recommended and must always include directions for the recipient to unsubscribe. Sending spam mail may get you into legal trouble; different jurisdictions have different laws, so be especially mindful if you sell across state or international lines. Consult an attorney for more information.

HTML Email

Standard email messages are plain text, but can contain file attachments. Many email clients also allow HTML content to be received, so that the email looks more like a brochure when opened. You may not have realized that opening your mail client is like opening a mini web browser and anytime you open an HTML email the same process that your web browser goes through when building a web page from files on a remote server begins. The marked up content gets styles applied, and images still get downloaded separately. The only difference is that styles are often coded right into the HTML instead of putting them in a separate .css file like we saw in Chapter 2. This is usually an attempt to address inconsistencies in mail client rendering capabilities and helps keep your emails backward compatible. Unless you are a web designer, you won't have to worry about that.

HTML emails create a professional feel for all of your business correspondence. If you would like HTML emails for your business, it's probably best to use some of the mailing list services with premade templates created by professional designers. This is because crafting good HTML emails that work well across all mail clients is a serious chore. Most professional templates also contain code that provides a plain text fallback for mail clients that do not support HTML emails. Also, most email clients do not let you simply drop in HTML content (other than links and images), so in those cases you have to use a third party server solution.

Mail Forwarding

Many domain registrars provide a free mail forwarding service with the purchase of a domain. This allows you to create a general email address, such as contact@trueanomaly.com, and have any mail sent to the address forwarded to any other address you specify (most likely your private email account). This is perfect for any scenario where you do not need to respond to the message (as the response will come from your private email account, which may appear unprofessional).

Figure 3-1 shows the process of setting up a mail forwarding account.

Figure 3-1 Setting up a mail forwarding account in Google Domains requires creating an email you would like to receive mail on, and a fully functioning account to which the mail will be forwarded.

If you want to respond to messages using an email address from your domain, then you need to pay for an email service such as GSuite and configure it for your domain. This is discussed next.

GSuite and Other Mail Hosting Services

GSuite (https://gsuite.google.com) is like Gmail for businesses and provides similar functionality. If you register your domain with Google, setting it up is easy. If you choose a different registrar or email service, the steps will vary, but all involve setting your MX records values to the domain of the mail service servers. See Chapter 1 again for more background information on this and then the online help documentation should be a breeze.

Obviously there are other mail hosting services; virtually every web host offers them as well. You are free to check those out on your own.

Email Newsletter and Marketing Services

As mentioned earlier, some common email newsletter and marketing services include:

- **ConstantContact** (https://www.constantcontact.com)
- **MailChimp** (https://mailchimp.com)

These services offer a lot, including services like unsubscribe functionality, HTML email templates, campaign management, opening and click-through tracking (to monitor the success of your campaign), and more. Some of the services may offer plug-in integration to your CMS of choice to sync contacts with accounts on your site.

Spam Filters

Email service providers are constantly trying to provide the best service to their clients. As such, they take aggressive measures to limit spam. These may include rating other email servers' reputability, including the servers your site uses to send email. To limit the amount of spam and help keep users secure, most email providers have an automated spam filter which screens messages for common patterns associated with unsolicited, fraudulent, and / or malicious emails. Unfortunately, these filters sometimes block legitimate attempts to reach a customer, such as transactional emails. Because of this, it is helpful to know just a bit about what spam filters look for in order to help our messages get through.

Much of fraudulent or malicious spam uses domain spoofing, which is when the email is sent from a different server than the one from which it claims to be sent. Email servers can claim to be any domain they want, but spam filters can look up the DNS MX record for the domain, and if the domain listed does not match the domain from which the message came, then the message is blocked. Unless you are a hacker, you won't be spoofing your domain intentionally, but setting these records properly to match your CMS email servers is important. Your email provider (such as GSuite or mailing list service) provides configuration steps to ensure that your DNS records match properly.

If utilizing a service such as GSuite to send manual emails, the automated emails that come from your CMS (such as transactional email), or the newsletter emails that some from a third party mailing list service, will have to come from a different domain. Typically, you will use a subdomain of your root domain such as mx.example.com. Remember that subdomains can have completely different DNS records than the root domain, but they are still set on the zone file of the root domain. Figure 3-3 shows setting an MX record for a fictional subdomain mg.trueanomaly.com.

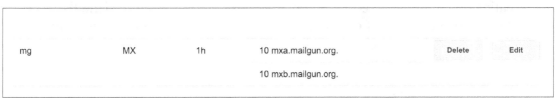

Figure 3-3 If the MX record for the domain doesn't match the server from which the email was sent, some spam filters may filter it to junk mail. This record shows the subdomain mg of a domain used to send transactional emails using an email service. Subdomains can have different DNS records including MX records than the parent domain.

The exact algorithms used by spam filters vary and many are proprietary, but we can guess some of the things they might look for. Some filters specifically screen for emails that appear to come from mailing lists, and some may even block anyone who is not in the user's contacts, even if those emails are solicited and legitimate. If your users tend to delete your emails without opening them, or mark them as spam consistently, their server may downgrade your emails to a lower priority or junk folder. There's nothing you can do about that except to always send relevant emails with engaging content and catchy subject lines. There is much more to learn about improving email **deliverability**. Do a web search for more information.

Review

We talked about the three main types of email a business can send to clients, and the concerns with each. We then looked at mail forwarding, and saw how to set it up for a domain. We then talked about setting up GSuite, by configuring our domain records properly (using one click in this case). We then looked at HTML versus plain text emails, and the concerns of each. Finally, we looked at spam filters and talked a bit about improving deliverability. By setting the MX records properly for our CMS generated and newsletter emails, we can help ensure that our emails don't end up in the users' junk folder. Multiple email services may require us to define MX records for multiple subdomains of our domain.

Lastly, creating engaging email content may help keep our emails out of the trash bin or spam folder, and over time that could improve the reputability of the server that sends our emails.

Chapter 4
Search Engine Optimization

Search engine optimization (SEO) refers to methods a website owner / operator can use to get a better **organic** or **local** ranking on search engines (i.e. have the link to their site appear closer to the top of the results for a particular keyword). Organic ranking refers to the order returned by the search engine algorithm. **Keywords** are the words or phrases used by people searching for your site. Everything in this chapter is general information for guidance only, and cannot guarantee a change in your site ranking on any specific search engine, but applying these tips properly may significantly boost your ranking over a site that has no optimization applied.

Search Result Organization

There are three areas to the results of web searches: paid, local, and organic. The paid listings are often at or near the top of the results and are sponsored ads that companies pay for likely on a per click basis. Below that, local search results return the most relevant businesses based on the user location, which the search engine can guess based on the browser IP address. The last section is the organic listings section, which contains the listings the search algorithm deems most relevant with no preference to location or payment. SEO techniques in this chapter seek to make your website appear higher in both the organic and local sections. Later we will mention paying for top placement.

Once your site is indexed, the home page may appear in the results with multiple sub-listings for other pages on your site, such as About, Story, Contact, etc. The search engine generates these automatically. Other pages on your site may also rank for different keywords and appear on their own. Each page can have a separate rank for any given search term.

General Rules for Better Ranking

While the exact algorithms used by search engines are usually proprietary, there are some general rules assumed to aid in a website ranking. When optimizing a website always remember that a search engine is essentially a software robot. It can scan the URL and HTML content for patterns and follow links, but the software does not have the reasoning a human would in determining the ranking. This means there are no points for beauty and the capabilities to scan images for content are limited. Although, high quality (relevant) images may lead to better ranking in image searches and drive up traffic, assuming you set the image alt attributes (discussed later) properly.

The URL plays a big role in the ranking of a site. If your URL is your business name, this should help you assume the top spot for searches exactly equal to your business name. This leads to one SEO technique of creating **landing pages** on your site with parts of the URL containing specific keywords. For example, if you had an online store that sells vintage clothing, you might have the link to vintage tees be example.com/mens/t-shirts/vintage-t-shirts/. This URL is loaded with keywords that people might use if they are searching for men's vintage t-shirts. The structure of your web page URLs are created by the server that hosts your website, so unless you are a web developer or hire one, you will be dependent on the CMS you choose (such as Squarespace or Shopify) and the theme designers to create optimized URLs based on your product categories.

The importance of the URL also leads to the SEO technique of creating websites with domain names equal to specific keywords that are tailored to a specific product or service your business offers. For example, if your business offers a whole range of equipment rentals, you might create a site specifically for floor sander rentals, on a domain that includes those keywords. This is a rather extreme technique, and has additional domain and hosting costs, not to mention upkeep, so only use it if your separate service or product is a large enough part of your business to warrant it.

Sometimes people get the idea to have a keyword heavy domain simply forward to their website. For example, you might buy vintagetshirtsofdetroit.com and have it forward to example.com. Pages that simply forward to others will likely not rank high.

Backlinks are links from external sites to pages on your site. The more backlinks, the more relevant your content, theoretically. Therefore, search engines may use this number to gauge your site ranking. Having social media pages for your business that link back to your website helps this number. Getting mentions by bloggers or news media outlets also helps. Customer reviews on relevant consumer recommendation sites may contribute as well. Search engines frown upon paying people to post links to your site, as they view this as an attempt to fool their algorithm.

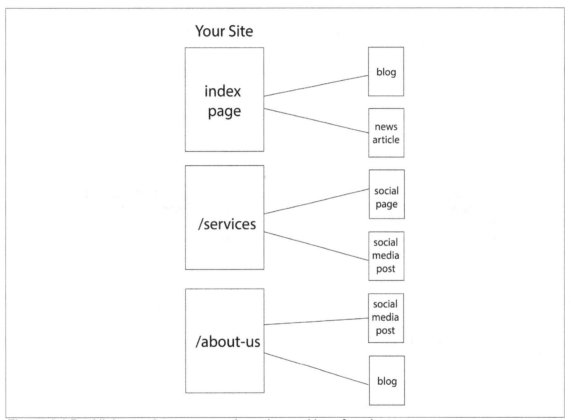

Figure 4-1 Backlinks can improve search engine ranking of each page.

Figure 4-1 shows some backlinks in action. Search engines are able to index other sites on the web and scan them for link tags (<a>) with an href attribute that contains your domain to determine this count. Sites are re-indexed periodically as their content and the number of backlinks changes.

As far as the HTML content is concerned, the title of the page in between the <title></title> tags is important. Packing page titles with keywords is a standard SEO trick, but be careful not to duplicate too many terms. Search engines may view duplicate content as spammy. In addition to the title tags, all header tags (h1, h2, h3, etc..) are likely scanned for keywords too. Loading header tags with relevant keywords is important, but make sure that the site remains usable to humans. Putting too many keywords in the header tags can lead to less relevant headers that may be confusing or awkward to your customers. Where the interests of the search bot and your customers collide, favor your customers.

```
<title>Example Company Tees | Vintage T-Shirts For Men and Women, Graphic Long Sleeve Shirts For Sale</title>

<h1>Men's Vintage T-Shirts</h1>

<h2>Graphic T-Shirts</h2>
```

Figure 4-2 Search engine friendly HTML title and header tags. The <title> tag is nested inside the HTML <head> tags at the top of the HTML file (document). The <head> tag is not to be confused with the header of the website, or content headers such as h1, h2, h3, etc tags. The <head> tag and its content (with the exception of the <title> tag) does not appear in the browser when the site is opened. The <title> tag content appears at the top of the browser window.

Figure 4-2 shows some HTML with search engine friendly page title and header tags. Your page titles should be unique on every page: do not duplicate titles. In addition to the title and headers, the content of the page itself (inside div and p tags) is also scanned. As a general rule, content near the top of the page may be weighted more than content later in the page.

Technical Stuff

In addition to the general rules, there are a few more technical tricks to search engine ranking. One is the speed at which your page loads. There are many things that advanced developers can do to improve the speed of page loading, unfortunately, if you are relying on code written by others (such as when using a CMS) all you can do is make sure your images are optimized. Adobe Photoshop has a nice "Save For Web" feature that may reduce the size of images substantially. Saving your images this way before uploading them to your website folder will cut down on page load times considerably. The same feature can be used to set the dimensions of the image. You can see how well the images are optimized by comparing the file sizes before and after the compression algorithm in Figure 4-3. Images on websites should have file sizes measurable in

Kilobytes (KB) rather than Megabytes (MB). This usually requires both compression and a reduction in the resolution (dimensions) of the image. However, because screens are small, this is usually not a problem for displaying on the web. You can always use a large desktop computer and expand the browser window wide to check if the image is distorting.

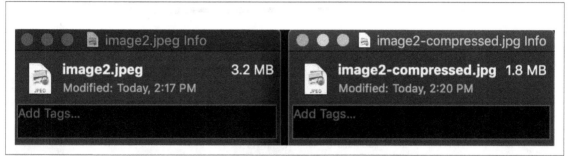

Figure 4-3 File size difference by running an image through "Save for Web". This reduction occurred with no change to the image dimensions, and fairly high quality. To get even more compression, reducing the resolution (the native dimensions of the image) or quality (more compression) you could easily get this photo file size to be KB.

An image file size is based on two factors: the native dimensions (resolution in pixels), and the quality of the compression. Lower resolution and higher compression lead to smaller, lower quality image, but a reduced file size. Choosing which (or both) of these factors to change is up to you. Reducing the dimensions is also known as cropping the image.

The web developer tools on a browser, mentioned in Chapter 2, have a profiler tool that shows the load times of each item on the site. You can use this data to figure out what is taking the most time and optimize it accordingly. A web developer will be required to take full advantage of this tool, but you can certainly optimize images using the techniques above. Also check graphics and icon files, although these may not reduce in size as much as images, make sure you aren't loading bigger files than are required to display properly. I have even heard of people saving their files (not just images, but CSS and JavaScript files) with single letter filenames (like x.png) to reduce the bits sent through the HTTP request! I can't say that that will help but it has been tried! Also see the Appendix for more information on images.

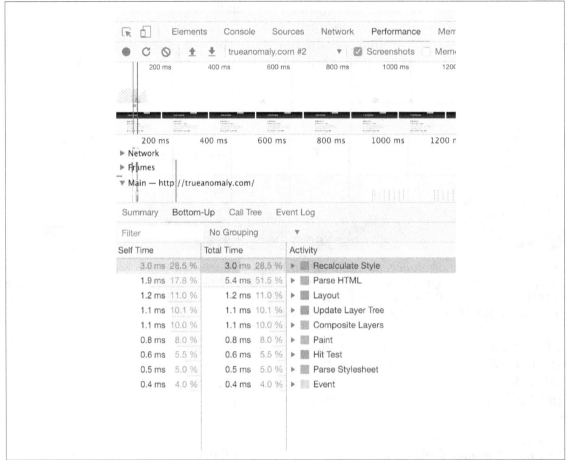

Figure 4-4 An analysis of the page loading by the developer tools performance tab.

Figure 4-4 shows web developer tools and the performance profiler tool that shows the loading time of each item on the page. If your CMS site loads slowly it could be a combination of poorly optimized content (that's your fault), a poorly optimized theme (that is the theme developer's fault), or poor hosting (that's the CMS provider's fault). At least you now know who to blame.

Our discussion of HTML in Chapter 2 barely scratched the surface of that large topic. There are many tags we never mentioned. One is the <meta> tag. It appears in the head tag of an HTML document and is probably not one of much interest unless you want to be a web developer. It can however, contain some keywords that some search engines may use to index the site. In addition, keywords about the content of images can be placed inside the alt attributes of img tags. Anything you type there will be read by screen readers and also appear on the page if the image fails to load. Those are the primary reasons for the alt attribute, however, search engines can also use it to index image content.

```
<img src="/images/climber.png" alt="a climber scales a rock wall outside Boulder Colorado" />

<meta charset="UTF-8">
<meta name="description" content="climbing gear and outdoor equitpment for sale ">
<meta name="keywords" content="climbing, gear, hiking, shoes, carabiners, outdoor, equipment">
<meta name="author" content="Nate">
<meta name="viewport" content="width=device-width, initial-scale=1.0">
```

Figure 4-5 An image tag with alt content and some useful meta tags. Meta tags are placed inside the <head> tag of the HTML document (each page of the website). Some CMS themes may generate these meta tags automatically.

Figure 4-5 shows meta and img tags with search engine friendly content. There are also meta tags for telling searchbots to not follow links and or ignore certain pages from the indexing.

There is also a specific HTML address tag for—you guessed it—addresses. It usually goes in the footer of your website. It is important to include it in order for search engines to place your site in local search results properly. Because the original use of this tag was for the author contact information, some theme developers may instead use an hCard format for the addresses. Most search engines should be able to read either. Look into your theme's HTML template footers and contact page to see if the address is marked up in some way that makes it computer readable. You'll also know if it's working if you show up in local search results and on Google Maps, although it may be some time after submitting your sitemap to search engines for this to display.

There are also specific meta tags to control the way your site appears on social media when someone shares a link to it on their platforms. These tags are called Open Graph meta tags, and the exact format depends on the social media platform you are targeting.

Check out these links for more:

Facebook (https://developers.facebook.com/docs/sharing/webmasters/)
Twitter (https://developer.twitter.com/en/docs/tweets/optimize-with-cards/guides/getting-started.html)

Some search engines may also use mobile friendliness of a page to gauge its ranking. Mobile friendliness refers to the appearance and ease of use of your website on small mobile devices such as smartphones and tablets. Unfortunately, unless you are a web developer there isn't much you will be doing to help this, as your mobile friendliness will depend on the theme you choose, but make sure you choose a theme that looks good on your smartphone! Also, know the the arrangement (order) of components and headers etc. on the page is under your control through the CMS, and this can affect the mobile friendliness of your site. Always test your site on a smartphone browser whenever you make significant changes to the layout, theme, or content. Even though the searchbot is a software robot, it may be able to tell if content is off the visible screen or jumbled, which is how it may gauge the mobile friendliness of your site.

Keyword Research

So we've learned the importance of keywords in the page titles, headers, meta tags, alt attributes, and content of our site. But how do we know which keywords to target? We can guess of course, but with analytics such as Google Analytics, we can see the search terms that people used to find our site. Using this data we can then search those terms ourselves to determine which keywords are highly competitive from our competitors and which might be slipping under the radar. If you search one and don't see your competitors near the top, then that would be a good keyword to target. We can find the under the radar search terms and load up our site with those to assume the top slot in a highly searched but less competitive set of keywords. See Chapter 7 for more about analytics.

Webmaster Tools

Webmaster tools are provided by the search engine companies to allow website owners to get a limited view of how the search robots view the their site. You can also submit a sitemap of your site to notify the search engine bot to index your pages. You don't want to submit your sitemap until your content is finalized and optimized. Although the search engines will index your site periodically, you will want your site optimized before the first scan.

Sitemaps are created in a format known as **XML**, which is a markup language with tags just like HTML. In fact, HTML is a subset of XML, but you don't need to worry about that. Major CMS providers create the sitemap for your site automatically and typically put it in a file called sitemap.xml. You can view it at example.com/sitemap.xml (where example.com is replaced with your domain). Each page to be indexed has a single entry on the sitemap.

For more information, check out these links:

Google (https://www.google.com/webmasters/**)**
Bing (https://www.bing.com/toolbox/webmaster)

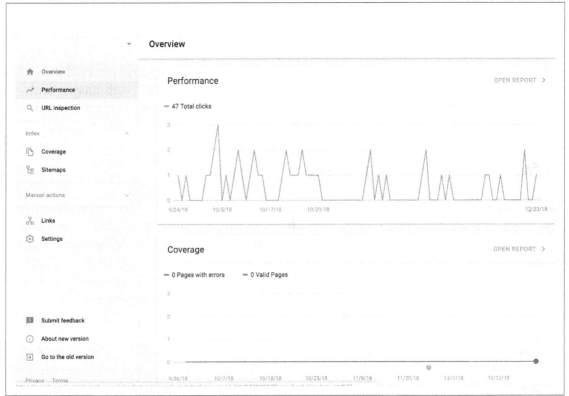

Figure 4-6 A screenshot of Google Search Console.

The tools also notify you of errors that occurred during the indexing of your site, and also have the ability to detect malicious content to an extent. Figure 4-6 shows a screenshot of the tools that display information about the number of pages indexed of a website. Google Search Console can also be linked to your Analytics account (discussed in Chapter 7).

Changing URLs

Anytime your change the URLs of pages on your site, your site may suffer a temporary search engine ranking drop. This is because search engines index your pages based on the URL, and if that URL leads nowhere (because the page was moved) it will eventually be dropped from the results. What changes URLs? If you switch CMS providers or delete or move page content to new pages, then the URLs change. To help guide the search engine, it is wise to have the server output an **HTTP 301 Permanent Redirect** to any clients that request the old URL. Web browsers will read that and automatically redirect to the new URL specified in the redirect. Your CMS may have a feature for creating these HTTP redirects; search their help files.

If you redirect a substantial number of pages, or the entire site (if you switched CMSs for example), it might be wise to purchase some search engine ads to help offset a dip in traffic once your site takes the temporary but inevitable hit to its organic ranking. Also make sure to update the sitemap.xml file and resubmit it through webmaster tools. It can take months for a completely redone site to regain its former position, assuming the new content is as optimized as the old content, and new backlinks to it form again.

Professional SEO Services

Chances are your business gets cold calls and emails from SEO services that promise to boost your search engine ranking. Should you utilize these services? The answer depends on how much money you have to spend, how much you value your organic ranking, and how much work you want to do yourself. The information in this chapter is very general; the tips here are provided as guidance only and do not guarantee any change to your web ranking. The tips in this chapter could be considered "common knowledge," as any SEO firm should know them and more.

The exact algorithms used by major search engines are not publically available, and they change from time to time. Theoretically, a professional firm keeps up-to-date on such changes, has real experience on what works and what doesn't, and can use that knowledge to increase your site ranking more than following the guidelines in this chapter. However, this depends on the quality of the firm you choose. Also, there is no reason why you cannot do your own research to keep up-to-date on changes and conduct your own experiments on your site to optimize it. As a result, the choice of using an SEO firm is completely up to you, but if you do choose to utilize their services, at least now you have some insight into what they might do, rather than blindly trusting their work.

Gimmicks

Naturally, some people like to deliberately fool search engine algorithms, so they use gimmicks. These are definitely not recommended, as search engines may look for them and can penalize your ranking if found.

Examples include:

- Text that matches its background color (to add keywords)
- Paid backlinks (paying for links to your site)
- Duplicate content or landing pages that duplicate content
- Excess keyword injection

Text that isn't visible to humans but is present for the searchbot, such as text matching its background color, is unacceptable. As mentioned previously, paying for backlinks to your site is frowned upon. Also, duplicating content across multiple pages or loading a page with lots of keywords over and over again could also harm your ranking.

Pay Your Way to the Top

As a last resort, you can always pay for your ads to be in the advertising section of the search results, which is at the top of the organic listings. There is considerable documentation online about how to best utilize these services (pick the right keywords, monitor your ad performance, etc). Check out the links below for more information:

Google Adwords (https://ads.google.com**/)**
Bing (https://bingads.microsoft.com/)

Review

In this chapter we looked at ways to improve our website's organic and local ranking in search engines. We learned a bunch of techniques, both general and technical, that can help. We also learned how webmaster tools can help us gain insight into our page, see what pages have been indexed, prevent certain pages from being indexed, and also submit our sitemap for indexing. We then learned about gimmicks that fool search engines and why to avoid them. Then we talked about the advantages of using a professional SEO firm. A summary list of techniques is below:

- URL
- Backlinks
- Title tags
- Header tags
- Page content
- Page speed
- Meta, address tags, img alt attributes
- Mobile friendliness
- Keyword research

Chapter 5
Social Media

Social media is an extremely important tool in the bag of any small business or startup. Social media helps cultivate **social proof**, which is the idea that when people see other people using your products or services (particularly people they know) they are more likely to use your business. Each social media platform offers a slightly different advantage to your business, although they all offer sponsored posts to targeted audiences. We won't discuss specifics of using the platforms here, as they are straightforward, well documented, and change frequently. Instead, we will discuss general techniques to better use social media to promote your business.

General Social Media Tips

Make sure your website contains links to your social media accounts, and vice versa, as links from your social media can count toward your backlink count if the searchbot is able to find them.

Your social media pages each have unique URLs, and you copy and paste those URLs into the appropriate place in your CMS. Almost all CMS themes incorporate custom designed social media links, and all you have to do is specify the URL for each link. People may not want to browse back to your homepage to find your social media account, so put these links in the footer of your site so they are visible on every page.

Your analytics (discussed in Chapter 7) can show you the social media referrals that are taking people to your site. From this data you can gauge your performance on each social media channel and also determine which is the largest driver of traffic.

Respond to your customers' messages or comments. Laziness can lead to ignoring messages, particularly if those messages do not indicate a high likelihood of a sale. It may seem like common sense, but it's worth saying that higher responsiveness may give a positive impression of your company's reliability. Social media platforms may gauge your responsiveness, and Facebook actually presents the response likelihood percentage to users.

Also, put like, share, send, pin, or tweet buttons on all product, service, and blog pages of your website. The easier you make it for users to share your content with others, the more traffic you will likely gain. Your CMS may include these. If not, check out the social media company's developer documentation to learn how to drop the appropriate HTML and/or JavaScript code into your templates. See Chapter 6 for the links. Having users share your site is the ultimate tool for viral (free) growth. Some CMS providers or open source CMS may have widgets that allow your users to type in their friends' email addresses to share your site. Some widgets even have code that will ask the user permission to access their email contacts to share your site with everyone in their contacts!

Lastly, note that social media companies may have very strict rules about the display of their trademarks on your website, as well as the use of their services. Breaking the terms and conditions (e.g. following too many accounts within a particular time period) can get your account blocked.

Facebook Pages

Facebook (https://www.facebook.com) Pages are a great tool for business if your clients are from the general public. Facebook Pages let users view your responsiveness to messages or comments. You can also boost posts for a fee to get your posts in front of more than just your followers. In my experience, Facebook has been the most effective social media referrer to my sites based on my analytics data. While every business' experience will vary, I highly encourage your business to have a Facebook Page and post to it often.

Post colorful pictures or video content to attract your followers' eyes. In a crowded news feed it's tough to get your followers' attention, especially with purely textual content.

Also see Chapter 6 for tips to create engaging website content, many of which apply to creating Facebook Page content and posts.

Facebook also provides the Facebook Insights tool that gives analytics information for your Page including views, likes, clicks and other actions to measure user engagement.

Instagram / Twitter Tips

I've grouped together **Instagram** (https://www.instagram.com) and **Twitter** (https://twitter.com) tips because both platforms utilize hashtags and operate similarly. Unless you run a photography business, Instagram may not seem particularly relevant to your business, but it provides a place for your users to tag your products or photos of them using your services, which adds to social proof. You can also offer rewards to users who do so, which in turn might lead to more people doing so. Adding a link to your site on your Instagram profile also helps drive traffic to your site.

To increase your Instagram or Twitter following, using the following common sense tactics may help boost your followers, site traffic, and potentially, sales. If you're a millennial or younger, it's fair to say you probably already know all of the following tactics.

First, if you already have a personal account on these platforms, create an account for your business only. You can certainly tag your personal account in your posts, or vice versa, but keep your personal posts off of your business page. Your dog and/or baby pics should not be on your company page.

All of the following tips boil down to one thing: stay active on social media. This comes more naturally to some than others. I know that I have to remind myself to post on social media because it's not really my thing. Other people post too often. How often is the right amount? That depends, and it's a personal choice. Your followers want content, and social media posts have very short lifetimes (at least to stay at the top of recent lists). So post often, but not so often that the quality of your content degrades because you are running out of material. Keep all of your content relevant to your business, and make sure it is consistent in quality. See also Chapter 6 on branding, as your social posts should be consistent with your brand message.

What else do we mean by staying active? Like a lot of other users' content, comment on content, follow relevant brands or celebrities, share relevant content or your followers' posts and respond to feedback (comments customers put on your content). Staying active ensures your brand is on lists that people check such as: the likes or comments of a particular post, the followers of their favorite celebrity, etc. The more your brand appears in these lists, the more exposure you will get.

When posting content, use hashtags and locations to get your content in front of others who are posting similar content, or those searching for such content. Many people follow particular hashtags or locations, so they help get your content in front of the right people. How many hashtags should you use? People disagree on the best number, but use as many as you want. Note however, that spam accounts use a lot of hashtags, and you don't want to look like a spam account.

As mentioned, these are just common sense strategies based on the nature of social media. Social media companies rely on the collection of data to better serve ads and make money. If you pay them, they can use this data to find your exact target audience and really dial in your social media presence. Just don't blow all your money on social media ads without seeing a return!

LinkedIn

If your business is primarily engaged in business-to-business transactions, getting through to movers and shakers is essential. These people can be tough to locate, and Facebook or other social media platforms are not necessarily the most appropriate way to locate people for business relationships. **LinkedIn** (https://www.linkedin.com) offers targeted ads and the ability to share your website blog posts that users in your network can like and share. This can make them more effective at reaching your audience than your website alone, which may or may not reach anyone new. LinkedIn can also be an effective tool to find and recruit employees, and network with other industry professionals.

Review

We learned the importance of social media for promoting your website and adding social proof to your products or services. We saw how Facebook is very effective for businesses that market products or services to the general public, and LinkedIn is effective for business to business marketing. We also learned some tips for Instagram and Twitter and general social media best practices to increase likes, followers, and overall customer engagement.

Using social media is straightforward; the sites have ample documentation to teach how to utilize their services, and that is why this chapter was so brief. With the right tactics however, it can become a potent tool for driving sales to your online business.

Chapter 6
Website Design

In addition to optimizing our site for search engines, we also want to optimize our site for visitors, after all, humans are the ones spending money! This requires special emphasis on design, branding, and content to increase client trust. Remember, your website must convince your customers that you can deliver as promised.

The most important thing: make sure your customers, immediately upon arriving at your site, can determine:

- Who is this brand
- What am I buying
- What is the theme of this brand (a one sentence slogan or tag line describing who the target audience is)

Brand Message

When people visit your website, they should immediately gain a clear understanding of what your brand is and what it represents. You communicate this with the theme you choose, the fonts, the color pallete, the logo, the images on home page, and your business slogan. It may be helpful to explicitly state this tag line right on the home page.

Customers need to identify with your brand before they will buy. This identification can only happen if the identity target or group of your customers is immediately obvious from the content on your home page.

When choosing a CMS theme, don't just pick the best looking one. Remember that every feature of it says something about your brand. Parallax effects (where the user scrolls down to reveal background content) are in vogue at the moment, but also can feel a bit gimmicky, and might even be frustrating to some users who feel like they're being herded and only shown what the site creator wants them to see. I think this feels like a very curated experience designed to lure you in with flashiness but is constraining. On the other hand, static sites without carousels or parallax effects may appear more traditional, but also allow the user to browse anywhere they want without feeling guided, and done properly, may also convey a sense of stability and reliability. Compare the sites of large publicly traded companies, as well as those of startups, and decide on which end of the spectrum your brand falls.

These are my opinions, and opinions differ. I know people that love the parallax design. But regardless of your opinions on design, remember that some people may only be visiting your site to get your address, hours, or phone number, and it can be frustrating to be forced into a guided tour when you just want to make a phone call. I believe that all websites should balance the goal of impressing users with the goal of usability.

Design for the Goal

Is the goal of your website to have the customer make a phone call? If so, make sure the design you choose features your phone number big and prominent. Is the goal of your website to have the customer make a purchase? Then make sure the home page features some of your products that they can access with a single click. This method is called building a clear **call to action**. Figure 6-1 shows a web page with clear calls to action. Calls to action typically consist of a clickable image link, a button, and one sentence description of the action. Perhaps nothing is more frustrating than seeing a picture of a product you want and not being able to click on it to learn more! Don't make your customers search, just let them point and click whatever attracts their eye!

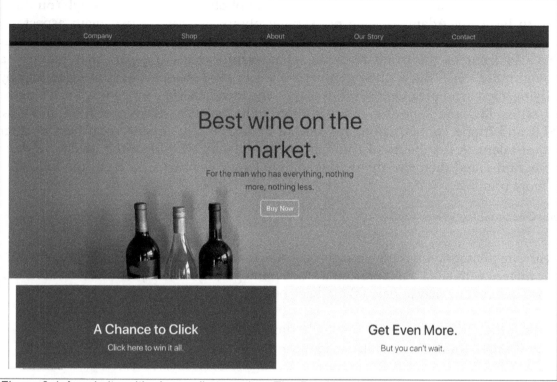

Figure 6-1 A website with clear calls to action. The Buy Now button in the center, with explanatory text above, as well as the two callouts below the hero image prompting the user for clicks. Although there is certainly plenty to criticize about this site, it is easy to determine in seconds the company sells wine for the man who has everything, and we should Buy Now!

Images that Sell

Business photography is all about the people. People often appear in business photography more than the products or services offered. This is because images of products or services without people can make your customers doubt whether your business is capable of what is advertised, or whether it even exists. Also, customer reviews without pictures are not nearly as believable as customer reviews with a name, picture, and date of purchase. That is social proof at its best.

Even though you want to feature people in nearly all your images, it is also important to have images of your products alone, with no distracting background. This can be accomplished with some work in Adobe Photoshop, or with a small studio photography light shed. Check out this one: (https://www.bhphotovideo.com/c/product/1032649-REG/impact_dls_j_digital_light_shed_48x48x48.html).

If you can't afford a photographer, learn to take photos yourself! Seriously! You don't have to be Ansel Adams to take marketable photos. There are two main aspects to learning photography: the technical side, and the composition side. Composition is what's in front of the camera (in the photograph), that's the part that requires a photographer's eye. But a photographer's eye can be developed with practice and by studying good examples. On the other hand—the technical side—meaning focal lengths and ratios, ISO and exposure compensation, light metering, flash operation and gels, DSLR and tripod configuration, etc. can all be learned by anyone regardless of their natural talent. A few hours of training can completely transform the quality of your photographs, and therefore the marketability of your website! Check out the following for more training:

KelbyOne (https://kelbyone.com)

If learning photography is not your thing, you can hire a local photographer or combine your images with stock images from a stock photography outlet. Just don't use all stock images or your site may appear fake. Check out the following:

Shutterstock (https://www.shutterstock.com)
Getty Images (https://www.gettyimages.com)

Keep Content Fresh

Updating content regularly (even if it's just the home page) is very important. Also make sure the copyright date at the bottom of your page stays current. Having it say a year older than the current year is tacky and can make customers wonder if your site is legitimate.

Page Speed

Page loading speed isn't just about SEO. People have little patience for slow loading sites. Utilize the tips in the SEO section for speeding up your page and make sure to test your site on mobile devices as they tend to be slower than desktop computers. If it takes more than five seconds to load your site you should find a way to speed it up. Cut down the number of images or the image sizes (as mentioned in Chapter 4) and consider moving video content to modals windows or have it loaded after the user clicks a link to it.

Remember Responsive Design

Make sure to view your site on mobile devices and tablets and laptops. These different screen sizes will render your page differently and it must be navigable and just as effective on all of them. For example, on a laptop, the screen height is usually shorter, which means that the content at the top of the page may fill their entire screen. Users may not even know that there is content below it, so don't count on any content below (content not visible unless the user scrolls) to get the user to do anything. In other words, don't expect the user to scroll to your calls to action or tag lines. They may not even realize scrolling is an option unless there are text or graphic (arrow) cues visible to suggest it.

The suggestion at the beginning of this chapter about your customers being able to immediately determine your product and why they should buy needs to be satisfied on all devices and screen sizes.

Ease of Navigation

Some of your site visitors will want to explore your whole site before making a purchase to get a sense of who your company is and the range of products or services you offer. It is important that your site be clearly navigable. This means using a consistent theme throughout (with the exception of the checkout page, which should be familiar to other checkout pages on commonly visited sites). It also means that all pages should have the same navbar at the top, and footer at the bottom, that is mobile friendly and consistent between pages. Don't make the user use their browser back button. It also means that you should not have pages that duplicate content or provide content similar enough that it might confuse the end user. If you offer one product, don't have two different product pages for the same product unless it's very clear on why they are different and they link to each other, for example.

Creating Content

In Chapter 4 we talked about the importance of content for search engine ranking. How do we create engaging content that will drive up our ranking? Once you create pages that describe all of your services, you may run out of content ideas. First, start by creating pages that do not specifically advertise your specific services, but instead inform and educate the customer about your business sector, the history, what advances have been made, what cutting edge research is focusing on, etc. These informational articles may draw more traffic than your promotional pages.

Often websites feature a blog for communicating news in your industry. Many CMS themes incorporate a blog for this reason, and as mentioned in Chapter 5, you may find that promoting your blog on LinkedIn or Facebook gains a bigger audience.

Increasing Customer Confidence

One big obstacle to getting sales is convincing your customers that your site is legitimate and trustworthy. Often people who otherwise like your products may not buy because they are afraid you won't deliver on your promises. Thus it is extremely important that your website convince people of your trustworthiness. Some techniques to increase the reputability of your site include:

- Better Business Bureau links
- Green address bar
- Customer reviews
- Photos of people with your products/services
- Clear privacy/return policies
- About us, our story, credits and history pages
- Customer logos
- Obvious and legitimate contact information

We already mentioned the importance of people in your site photos and social media for increasing social proof.

Figure 6-2 A green address bar in Firefox. The verified company name is displayed to the left of the URL along with a lock. Different browsers may display it differently, not all use green color.

You can also get a green address bar in some browsers (see Figure 6-2), which can convey a sense of trustworthiness to customers. This requires buying an **Extended Validation** SSL certificate. You may remember we talked about HTTPS in Chapter 1. Any reputable CMS should setup the secure connection automatically, but you may have to pay more to get extended validation, from a Certificate Authority. Check with your CMS for more information about how the implement this.

Also check out the following link on extended validation:

Thawte (https://www.thawte.com/ssl/extended-validation-ssl-certificates/)

The Better Business Bureau also offers links that you can put on your site that your customers can click to verify. Check out this link for more:

BBB (https://www.bbb.org/become-accredited)

Make sure your privacy policy, return policy, and terms and conditions are clear and easy to find on your site. Perhaps nothing turns off customers quicker than a shady or non-existent return or service cancellation policy. See the end of this chapter for more recommendations on the content of privacy policies and terms of service.

Having real customer reviews with small pictures of the customers themselves, with their permission of course, is a wonderful tactic to increase customer trust. Social media platforms have ways of displaying a user's friends who like or share content on your site, as long as that user is logged into their platform when they view your site.

Check out the following links:

Facebook (https://developers.facebook.com/docs/plugins/share-button/)
Pinterest (https://developers.pinterest.com/docs/widgets/save/**?)**
Twitter
(https://developer.twitter.com/en/docs/twitter-for-websites/tweet-button/overview.html)

Finally, the importance of an About Us or Our Story page cannot be overstated. Having the names and photographs of the business owners and employees can make a huge difference in the reputability of your company. It is often good to use round edges on the photos, or circular photos, as round edges appear friendlier and approachable. This can be achieved with the CSS style (border-radius: 10px) applied to the img tags. Scam websites do not tend to put names and pictures on them. Credits and history pages can be used to show off your previous work. The brand message and story of the founders play off each other to make the sale. Don't just tell customers why they should buy, always answer the question, "why are you selling this?" Why is the most important question to answer!

If your work is primarily business to business, and you get permission to do so, including the logos of your customers in a big group on the home page can do wonders for credibility, especially if your customers are recognizable brands.

Finally, the simplest thing you can do to increase customer confidence is provide obvious and clear contact information for your business. Don't just present a contact form to fill out. Publish an address with a map, phone number, and email address. A published email address will undoubtedly receive a lot of spam mail, as spam bots scour the Internet for such things. Thus, you should use a generic email that your create specifically for this purpose, such as contact@ or support@ or sales@. The increase in spam may well be worth it, as your customers will likely feel much more comfortable with real contact information visible.

Importance of Branding

While not specifically a website tip, the importance of branding your business also cannot be overstated. Branding refers not only to making your business convey a clear message with a tag line or slogan, but ensuring the logo and tag line communicate the same message. Also keep your website graphic design is consistent with all of your print and in-person branding (invoices, letterheads, notepads, pens, hats, etc). These techniques make your business seem less "small-businessy." Even if you're deliberately going for a "not corporate" look—such as hand written chalkboards—this look can be consistently applied across your web and print materials. Consistency is key to trustworthiness, and trustworthiness is important even if your brand is not trying to feel corporate. Your social media accounts may be the first exposure your clients have to your brand. The content on them should be consistent with your website and print publications as well.

Favicons

The favicon is the small icon that browsers display next to the address bar. It also displays when someone bookmarks your site. Adding a favicon adds a bit of professionalism to your site, and it is easy. Simply put a 16px X 16px or 32px X 32px size image named favicon.ico, favicon.png, or favicon.jpg in your website folder. Different CMS's may also provide a method for you to do this, but simply uploading the image to your web folder should work, as browsers look for this file automatically. Historically, this image was a .ico file and older browsers only support that file type. This should not be an issue in modern browsers: they accept .png and .jpg types.

Obviously, the file extension should match what type of image file it is, so don't just change the extension, resave the file with a photo or graphic program as the appropriate file type (probably PNG-24). Figure 6-3 shows a favicon.

If you want an ICO image, or want to learn more about favicons, check out this question:

Stack Overflow (https://stackoverflow.com/questions/4014823/does-a-favicon-have-to-be-32x32-or-16x16)

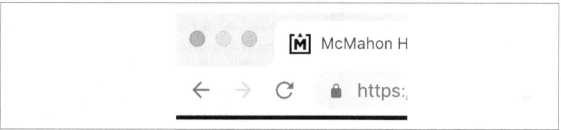

Figure 6-3 A browser favicon appears in the tab or the address bar depending on the browser. It also appears next to bookmarks.

A/B Testing

A/B testing is a great way to fine tune your website into a sales machine! The idea is that you launch two different versions of your website (same products/services, but different themes). Then you use analytics tools like Google Analytics (see Chapter 7), or the built-in tools from your CMS, to track which version leads to better sales. Using this method over and over as seasons change you can dial in your website as an optimized, year-round sale converter!

Custom sites (not CMS sites) could be coded so that the versions would rotate (A shown to every other user, B shown to every other user). If you are using a CMS, you probably don't have to option to do that. Instead, you will create your site using two different themes, and change it manually after a specified period (maybe 1-3 days), and then analyse the traffic with analytics tools to see which theme performed better.

The concept of A/B testing can also be used on emails, as email newsletter and marketing services will often allow you to view conversions (email opening and click through rates to your site). This allows you to optimize your promotional content as well.

Focus Groups

Focus groups are a tool used by startups to test the viability of their products on people. They can also be used to determine if your website is communicating the message you want to communicate. Get some unbiased reviewers together, show them your site, and ask them how it makes them feel and what they perceive. This will let you know if your design is succeeding in its goal.

Accessibility

There are things a theme designer can do to ensure that a site is accessible to screen readers and individuals with disabilities. There are standards that have been developed to achieve the objective of improving the accessibility of the web to all users. A theme that has been designed in accordance with these standards may advertise itself as conforming to WAI-ARIA standards. Contact your theme developer for more information on the conformity of your chosen theme. For more information on WAI-ARIA, check out this link:

W3C (https://www.w3.org/WAI/standards-guidelines/aria/)

Abandoned Shopping Carts

Some websites utilize cookies to track down users who put items in a shopping cart and left the site and invite them to return to the site through email. Depending on how you implement this, the technique may only email those who have created an account and logged into your site, or it may use third party cookie tracking software to identify users. Receiving unsolicited emails after browsing a site can be a little unsettling, so look into such services only if you feel strongly about them.

Shopify Blog (https://www.shopify.com/blog/12522201-13-amazing-abandoned-cart-emails-and-what-you-can-learn-from-them)

Privacy Policy and Terms and Conditions

It is essential that your site displays a clear Privacy Policy and Terms and Conditions. These may even be required by law.

You should consult an attorney for the proper wording of these. Some suggested privacy policy content is listed below:

- What data your site collects
- How you use that data
- To whom you share that data
- How data is stored and for how long
- Your use of browser cookies
- Your customers' data rights
- Third party software on your site such as analytics or mapping software with links to any applicable privacy policies or terms and conditions

The last point is important. If your site embeds a map from a mapping service such as **Google Maps** (https://www.google.com/maps), that service may place additional cookies on the browser. Any third party software you embed in your site could potentially place cookies on your user's browsers and they need to be made aware of this. See Chapter 7 for more about analytics.

If your CMS site allows customers to login, then you are collecting their email addresses. Since you do not own the servers that host your site—in fact, your CMS provider may not even own them as such services are often hosted on cloud servers—you are potentially making this data visible to the staff of the company that does. You ought to disclose this, and make it clear your policy, as well as the policies of any technical providers.

As far as terms of service, they should define proper uses of your site as well as improper uses of your site, and include at least the following:

- Disclaimer and limitation of liability statement
- Trademarks and copyrights
- Any other notifications or disclaimers recommended by your attorney

Not only do thorough polices and terms of service help protect you from legal issues, they also can serve to enhance customer confidence, as taking the time to display clearly worded and comprehensive policies suggests legitimacy.

Strong Passwords and Two-Factor Authentication

Although not a design tip, the security of your site is still of utmost importance. One data breach could easily kill your company. If you have not used two-factor authentication to help secure your personal online accounts, the time has come. As a business owner, your website will hold account information on other users, so you must take every measure appropriate to guard their data. This means using a strong password and enabling two factor authentication which sends a code to your phone or email that you need to login. A good way to create a strong password is a passphrase, which is using the first letter of each word in a phrase you commonly use and can remember such as "my favorite season is fall for the pumpkin spice," which leads to the password "MFSIFFTPS".

The monetary consequences for exposing customer data can be severe. While you may have been lax about your personal account security in the past, your business accounts cannot be treated so lazily. If you are a larger organization with many employees, consider creating a written company security policy detailing procedures for the access, control, and handling of customer and company information, as well as customer notification procedures should the worst happen. As always, consult an attorney for information on liability in the event of a data breach. See the Appendix for more.

Keep Up-to-Date

Like fashion, web design trends change. You need to keep up on these changes particularly if you are in a trendy industry. There are thousands of blogs dedicated to that sort of thing. Here's one site you might check out:

Smashing Magazine (https://www.smashingmagazine.com)

Review

In this chapter we learned how to increase the effectiveness of our website. We learned to design for the goal, whether the goal is to get the customer to make a phone call, or place an order online. We learned the importance of calls to action, branding, and how fonts, colors, images and other content all communicate something to our customers. We learned the importance of applying these principles to our site on all devices, including smartphones and tablets. We the learned about using A/B testing to dial in our website for increased conversions. Finally, we looked at ways of increasing customer confidence in our website.

Chapter 7
Analytics and Other Tools

This chapter will briefly discuss web analytics tools and how they work. We will not discuss the specifics of using any particular company's tools, because these features change often, but we will learn enough background information that online documentation will be clearer.

Analytics

Analytics are small snippets of JavaScript code provided by search or CMS companies that get copied and pasted into your site and allow you to gain insights into the traffic on your site. The analytics code can tell the browser the customer used to access your site, their approximate location (based on the IP address), the search term they used to find your site (if applicable), the page they landed on first, and links they clicked, and also the referrer (the website that linked to yours).

Analytics are also built into some CMS, but third party analytics such as **Google Analytics** (https://analytics.google.com/analytics/web/) may offer more tools and insights. Using this data, analytics can show which pages draw the most customers initially, and also give a view of their use of site. You can use this information to better optimize the content of your site for usability (to increase sales), and also to enhance its SEO.

Third party analytics may want to verify that you own the domain you are going to track. Often this involves placing a TXT record on your DNS zone file. Chapter 1 should give you enough info to do this with ease. The URL for your property is the home page of your site, which is just your domain name with or without the www subdomain (depending on how you setup your DNS records). To check which you did—in case you don't remember—type in your domain in your browser and see if it automatically prefixes it with www or not when you press Enter. Whichever displays in your address bar is what you should name the property.

To use third party analytics you will need to grab the tracking code they provide and drop it into your CMS in the proper location. Most CMS provide such a location as it is common to use third party analytics code. Notice that the code is linked to your HTML through a script tag in the HTML header.

A notice of the use of analytics tools should be included in your privacy policy and terms and conditions, even if you are only using the analytics provided by your CMS. This is not legal advice. More information can be found at the link below if you are using Google Analytics, but as always, consult an attorney for the proper wording of your site Privacy Policy and Terms and Conditions.

Google Analytics (https://www.google.com/analytics/terms/us.html)

Once you have verified ownership of a domain and dropped the tracking script tag into the proper place, you should be able to receive data on your analytics. Analytics can be used for a variety of business goals:

- View the number of site visitors in real-time
- Analyze traffic flow through your site
- Determine the effectiveness of different page content through A/B testing
- Determine which landing pages are the most effective
- Determine the location of your site visitors
- Determine how traffic is getting to your site
- Determine the effectiveness of your social media accounts
- Determine which search terms to use to optimize your site

Analytics are essential to gauging how well the SEO techniques in Chapter 4, and the social media tips in Chapter 5, and the user optimization techniques in Chapter 6, are performing. By monitoring traffic to, from, and through your site, you can dial in your content to drive visitors from social media and increase the ratio of sales to visitors. Any links on other sites (social media pages or otherwise) are called **referrers**, as they refer visitors to your site. JavaScript code, mentioned in Chapter 1, can access the domain of the link that brought them to your site, so that's one way the tracking code gets this data.

Pay attention to a page's **bounce rate**. This number tells you the percentage of users who drop off after viewing a certain page. If a page, especially the home page or a landing page, has a high bounce rate, it could indicate that that page is not doing a good job of selling your product or service, or could indicate that the ads or social media links that arrive there are misleading users as to the content of that page. Also take a look at the flow of users through your site to determine if your site is engaging them. The more pages they visit before leaving, the better.

This is just a brief overview of what is possible with analytics tools. All of the aforementioned business goals can be achieved without much learning, but there are entire courses dedicated to analytics. These courses will teach you how to integrate your analytics with your paid ads and manage campaigns, as well as develop in depth views to visualize specific data. There are also tools that analyse user activity across multiple platforms such as smartphones and apps. You can check these courses out to learn more about these features if you desire:

Google Analytics Academy (https://analytics.google.com/analytics/academy/)

Sell on Amazon, Google for Retail

If your site gets more traffic than Google or Amazon, then you really didn't need to buy this book. Since it probably doesn't, you can leverage some of their resources by creating storefronts on their sites. Creating an Amazon storefront can supplement your own website by selling to people who are already logged into and using Amazon.

For more information, check out these links:

Google for Retail (https://www.google.com/retail/)
Amazon Services (https://services.amazon.com/content/sell-on-amazon.html)

Other Services

There are many other business services offered by a variety of companies as plugins to the various CMS systems. Each of these services can cut down on the amount of busy work you need to do to run a successful small business.

Bookkeeping integration can allow your online storefront to "talk" to your bookkeeping software to cut down on the amount of entering sales manually.

Customer relationship management plugins can help you manage and track your communications with your customers by automatically creating customers from accounts created on your storefront and tracking email and newsletter contact.

Order fulfilment allows your storefront to stock your products at a warehouse (usually following specific packing instructions) so that they can accept orders electronically from your storefront, pick them and ship them for you.

Review

In this chapter we learned about the importance of analytics tools to view our site's traffic and demographics. We learned how to view the referrers to our website, and how to use this information to enhance our SEO. Then we briefly mentioned tools that make our lives as small business owners easier.

Congratulations

You made it! You now know enough about the Internet and the web to launch an online business with confidence. If you encounter terminology that you still do not understand, search the term and chances are good forums or blog posts will hold the answer. Hopefully this book has served its purpose and has given enough background that such posts and help files will not seem so cryptic. Good luck!

APPENDIX
Miscellaneous Topics and Tips

This Appendix includes exposition of an assortment of related topics that may assist you in running your online business.

Choosing a CMS

In Chapter 2 we discussed how a Content Management System is an online website builder program that allows non technical users to build a web page by uploading images and populating web page templates with content specific to their company. The very first decision you must make as a business owner seeking an online presence is which CMS to use. The considerations are cost, availability, quality, and applicability of themes, ease-of-use and features. Hopefully, this book provided enough information for you to feel comfortable using a domain registrar, pointing it at your site, setting up email and other tasks. If not, however, or if you don't want to deal with anything technical at all, choose a provider that offers those services built in. Some CMS providers do offer domain registration and configuration. You still may want GSuite (see Chapter 3), which means that configuring the DNS records might be a little trickier than if you registered your domain with Google. Some CMS may offer support or even automatic setup.

My advice is to consider the following:

- Which CMS is tailored to your use case (Shopify for online stores, for example)?
- Which CMS offers 24/7 phone support?
- Which CMS offers the best themes, including a large selection of third party theme designer themes?
- Which CMS allows for complete HTML/CSS customization?
- Which CMS offers a reasonable price?

Obviously, price may be the consideration that overrules the others, but if it isn't consider the use case and availability of quality themes first.

Payment Gateways

Often when browsing sites you may see it advertised that your credit card information "never touches" their servers. This certainly sounds reassuring, but what does it mean exactly? The Payment Card Industry governs the collection and storage of customer credit card information. The Data Security Standard set forth by the PCI is extensive and complex, and the simplest way to comply with it is by letting a qualified third party handle it. This solution is known as incorporating a payment gateway into your site. Let's take a look at how it works. Note: other methods have different workflows. They include PayPal, Apple Pay, Bitcoin and others, but we will not look at those here.

Your site hosts a credit card information form (served over HTTPS) that, when submitted, sends the payment info to a credit card processor for validation, in exchange for a token that represents the credit card (a.k.a payment source). Your site code then sends this token and a charge amount to your server, which combines this information with a private key (invisible to your customers) and uses that combination to create a charge and send it to the gateway. The gateway then processes the charge against the source created previously and returns the result (success or failure) to your server, which in turn pushes it out to your site (the client). Whew! Figure A-1 illustrates this process.

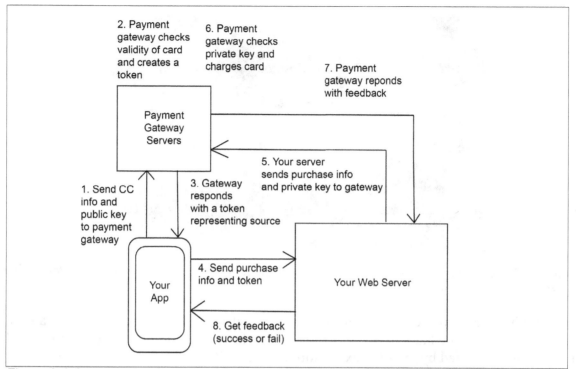

Figure A-1 A payment gateway workflow. The user's credit card information is never sent to your backend server.

Fortunately, most CMS for online storefronts setup and configure the payment gateway so you don't have to code up this workflow for yourself, but now you know what's going on.

Images

Every digital photograph (image) is composed of pixels, which are a combination of three color values (one red, one green, one blue). Each of these color values is represented by a number. To see the values of these for a particular pixel, and you have an Apple computer, open up the Digital Color Meter tool in Applications->Utilities and take a look. This is shown in Figure A-2.

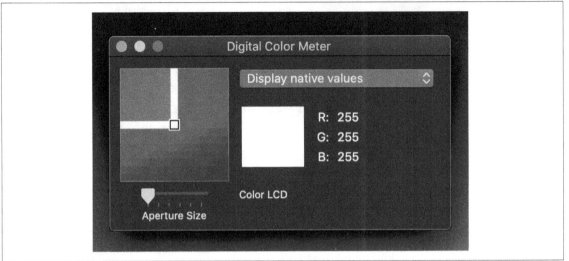

Figure A-2 The Digital Color Meter tool shows the RGB values of any pixel on your monitor as you move the mouse around.

Because images form such an important part of a website, it is important to know a little about them beyond what you may have learned so far. First, there are four main types of image files, indicated by their file extension (jpg, png, gif, tiff).

JPEG images are compressed with an algorithm specifically designed to eliminate unnecessary pixel color information without degrading the image too much (in other words, identify areas of the image with similar colors and eliminate duplicated information without degrading the image). Note that JPEG images created on iOS or Mac OS X may be given a .jpeg extension rather than a .jpg. You should change it to .jpg (just change the extension, no software conversion required) before putting it on the web as some browsers may not recognize .jpeg as a file type. PNG files are another common image format on the web.

PNG files can have transparent backgrounds which allow the background of the website to show through. This is nice for logo images for example, where the background color of the navbar should show through. With a .jpg image, the entire image has a background color, which, if different from the background color of the site, produces a colored box around the image.

GIF images are common for graphics and can also be animated by saving a series of individual images and having the browser rotate through them. This can add a bit of dynamic behaviour to a site, especially if the animations are triggered when scrolling the page. Search "creating animated GIFs" for more.

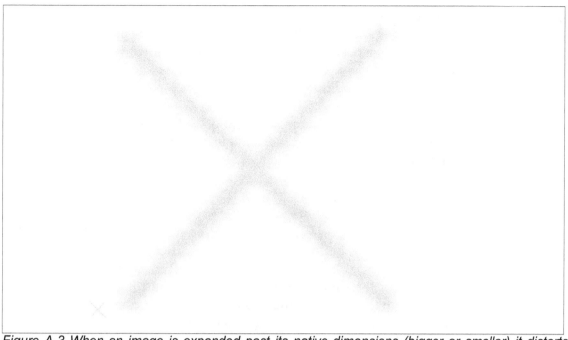

Figure A-3 When an image is expanded past its native dimensions (bigger or smaller) it distorts. When you see this on your website you need to either resize the native dimensions of the image in photo editing software (by cropping to specific size or getting a higher resolution image if you need it to be bigger) or change the dimensions it is displayed in browser by changing the CSS. Sometimes CSS (or even HTML attributes) specifies the exact width and height, but often the image is expanded to fit its container div.

All images have dimensions that are set when the file is initially saved. These dimensions are the **native dimensions**. Any file browser on your operating system should display the dimensions of an image when you highlight the file. If not, right click and select "Get Info" and scroll down. CSS can set the image dimensions too, either explicitly by hard coding values for height and width, or leaving it up to the browser by letting the image expand to the size of its parent container (which could change based on the size of the browser window/device width). If an image is expanded or shrunk to dimensions that are drastically different from the native dimensions, the image will be blurry.

In addition, if the **aspect ratio** (ratio of width to height) of an image is changed from its native aspect ratio, the image will be distorted. If you upload an image to your CMS and it appears blurry when you view the web page, it is probably because its image dimensions are being set by some CSS code, or (more rarely) hard coded as attributes in the HTML. If you really paid attention when reading Chapter 2, you might be able to locate the template file that is creating the HTML, as well as the CSS file that is styling it, using the browser developer tools. Seeing what image dimensions it is being scaled to, you can resave the image in proper dimensions (or at least very close dimensions) and then re-upload it to your server. Remember, changing the dimensions in the browser developer tools does *not* change the image dimensions for anyone else's browser, so you can't fix the problem that way, you must resize the image and re-upload it. Resizing images requires graphics or photo editing software.

Note: simply resaving the image in the proper dimension will not fix the issue. You may have to crop the image to the proper aspect ratio first using photo editing software. If it's a graphic, resave the file or export it as an SVG (see next) if you have the proper software.

Because of the problem of rendering images at the wrong size on different screens, whenever an icon or graphic image is used, it is better to use a **Scalable Vector Graphic** (SVG). These images are defined as computer instructions to draw the image, rather than discrete pixel color values. This is not the best way to display complex illustrations like pictures, but for simply icons (like those on buttons) it's perfect. SVG images scale automatically to their size, so there is no image distortion. To create SVGs, you need graphics software that can export the file. The process is too complex for this book, but web searches and the software help documentation can help.

Progressive Web Apps vs. Native Apps

At some point you may desire to create a mobile app for your business to increase customer engagement, retention, and do more business in general. If you do, you will need to employ a professional developer or hire a third party company to build the app for you. In either case, they may ask whether you desire a progressive web app or a native app. Both options have advantages and disadvantages.

A **progressive web app** (PWA) is essentially a website, only with more JavaScript code to make it function more like a program on your computer. That means instead of having separate pages for content, a PWA will be a single page application (index.html) that loads more content into it via JavaScript code. When a website is written this way, it is said to be a web app. Web apps can be stored on the home screen of smartphones and launched with a tap, just like native apps, but your customers may not know how to do this. The advantage is that they may be cheaper to build and are accessible by any device with a web browser.

Native apps are the apps you are probably familiar with. They are purchased from the App Store or Google Play Store and downloaded onto the smartphone hard drive. The advantage is that they work as expected by the user, as this is the workflow most people expect when you say, "try out our app." The disadvantage is that the company you hire to build a native app will have to code one version in Swift for iOS, and another version in Java for Android. Some companies may not have the developer talent to do this, and those that do will likely charge for each version of the app, which will add to the cost.

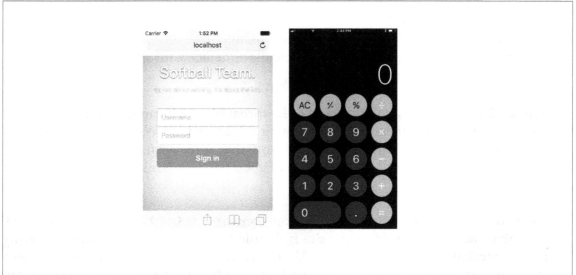

Figure A-4 A web application running inside a mobile browser and a native app (the Calculator app) running on iOS. A web application can have the browser address bar hidden and home screen icon with the proper meta tags added. Reprinted with permission, Learning to Build Apps, (2018 True Anomaly LLC).

Native apps may cost more, but they arguably provide the best look and feel and usability, which many consider desirable. This is because PWAs are subject to some web browser default behaviours and looks that may not be completely overridable by the developer. Also, push notifications work differently in PWAs and this may be undesirable.

Security

Many entrepreneurs are afraid of bringing their business online because of the fear of hacking. This is mostly a fear of the unknown. Without a clear knowledge of the threats, the possibility remains very scary. There are a number of attacks a hacker can launch at an online storefront. We will mention a few here, not in the hope that these brief descriptions will allow you to configure your servers to stop them, but rather to educate, so that you can have a better faith in your CMS service. The good news: Hollywood often exaggerates the ability of hackers to take over sites. Rule number one: keep your CMS secure with a good passphrase and two-factor authentication.

Here is a brief list of common attacks:

- Domain spoof (also a type of phishing)
- Man-in-the-middle
- Wire sniffing
- Cross-site-scripting (XSS)
- Phishing (email, or text, CSRF or social engineering)
- Stealing your CMS password (to get emails or deface your site)
- Denial-of-service attacks (DOS)

We talked about domain spoofing already, the threat of which can be lessened by using DNSSEC, a service you can enable through your DNS provider. We also explained man-in-the-middle and wire sniffing attacks and how that threat can be lessened by using HTTPS. We also mentioned the importance of good passwords, as password guessing is still a common attack vector.

Denial-of-service attacks occur when a hacker bombards your site with so many HTTP requests that the server hosting your site is unable to handle anymore, thus rendering your site unavailable to legitimate users. Unless you are hosting your site yourself (on a dedicated or cloud server) and are a trained server administrator, there is nothing you can do to prevent this attack. Your hosting provider can provide limited protection, if this attack occurs you can call them and complain. They may already know about it as their traffic will be spiking but they should be able to block the traffic if it is coming from one or just a few sources. There are such things as distributed denial-of-service attacks that use a growing array of servers that are much more difficult to stop, but these are not typically targeted at small business sites unless the neighbour you feud with happens to be a member of a group of skilled hackers. In summary, your site, as well as any other site on the web, is vulnerable to DOS attacks but the likelihood of an attack on your mom and pop site is fairly low.

Next let's talk about cross-site-scripting (XSS). XSS attacks are the result of a malicious user injecting JavaScript code into your site. This attack is possible if users (customers) have the ability to post content to your site, such as product reviews or comments on blog posts, or even their username. As a non-developer, you are trusting that the developer who wrote your customer review component or blog commenting widget escapes the output before it gets displayed on your site. It would be difficult to imagine a reputable developer forgetting this step, but it is possible. To test any of your components, type in the following code as a comment or user review:

<script>alert('Houston we have a problem');</script>

If a dialog pops up that says "The page says, 'Houston we have a problem'", then the input is not being escaped and an XSS vulnerability exists and you should contact your theme developer or CMS for support.

Note: this test is not applicable to inputs on the backend of your CMS when you login as a site administrator, such as the page creation inputs. These inputs may allow JavaScript or other tags as they are meant to be accessed by admins (you and your team only). The vulnerability we are tyring to prevent here is only applicable to inputs that are available to customers of your site (such as product reviews or comments). If a customer succeeds in getting into the admin portion of your CMS, your site is totally hacked already, the XSS almost becomes a moot point, as they can do whatever they want (deface your site, steal email addresses, etc.). That's why strong passwords and two-factor authentication are critical to prevent unauthorized access to your CMS. This is not the only attack vector XSS can use, but it is common.

You must keep your CMS theme up-to-date. Theme developers release updates to themes as they can contain vulnerabilities similar to what was mentioned above. If the theme developers find a vulnerability, they will release a fix for it and you must update ASAP. Many attacks are deliberately designed to take advantage of themes that have not been updated.

The final attack we will look at is an email or text message phishing attack. These can take may forms, but some rely on the same basic principle. They are generally trying to take advantage of you already being logged into a site (so they can run code that takes actions only you can take) or they are trying to get you to go to a page they have control of and get you to type in your username/password (which would otherwise be unguessable). Steps to mitigate this include: staying logged out of all websites until you have to do something that requires logging in, clearing your browsing cache and history frequently (or never storing history), and not clicking links in emails. Totally disabling cookies would help too, but that would make it impossible to login to most sites *ever*, which is not very practical. To screen for email phishing attacks, one technique—although not fool proof—is to verify the domain the email was sent from without opening the email. The procedure to do this varies from mail client to mail client, but often the domain gives you all the information you need. For example, if the message is posing as a message from some company, but a glance at the from address shows that the domain is misspelled or something close but not quite right, then you should be suspicious and not open it. It is true that sometimes companies use different domains to send emails, but misspellings are unlikely and you can always check with a company to see the domains from which they send legitimate emails. Also note that the "from" address cannot be trusted even if it appears legitimate, as a server can set this. Hopefully your email server catches this and filters this mail to spam if it does not match properly, but be vigilant anyway.

Disabling JavaScript can help prevent becoming the victim of an XSS attack, but this is not practical either, as web apps won't work without JavaScript. Some browsers also have a Java Runtime Environment built in. Java is not JavaScript, they are two completely different languages. Unless you frequently use websites that require it, you can safely disable Java in your web browser if your browser gives you the option to do so. Not having a Java Runtime Environment installed works just as well too. Adobe Flash is another technology used by some websites, but unless you frequently use those sites, you can safely disable it as well. In the security world, disabling things is called "keeping your attack surface small," and it's always a good idea.

There are many attacks not on the list here that are aimed at servers, but unless you are hosting your own site on a server, you can't do much to prevent them, except trust your CMS provider. If you chose a DIY CMS mentioned in Chapter 2, such as Joomla or Drupal, you must acquire a knowledge of threats related to LAMP servers. Like the XSS example shown here, many vectors involve attacking the inputs of your site (username field, password field, comment field, etc.), and also probing your server for inputs the server admin either overlooked or forgot to close.

There are obviously many more attacks than we discussed here, but these are the basics. In addition to keeping your site and customers secure, you must also take steps to keep yourself secure. Here are some more common sense rules to follow: stay logged out of sites whenever possible, don't run software downloaded from the Internet, disable unnecessary browser plugins, keep your browser up-to-date, don't click links in emails (copy and paste them into your web browser and check the domain of the site matches what you expect before hitting enter), don't enter sensitive information on any site that isn't served by HTTPS with a lock displayed in the address bar, be wary of email phishing schemes that prompt your for account information.

Generally, whenever faced with a shady link or download, don't take action. Take a breath and think before you click or type in your password. Although written for developers, check out this excellent resource for learning about web security, common vulnerabilities and hacks, and what to do if your site is hacked:

Google (https://developers.google.com/web/fundamentals/security/)

Relative URLs

There are two root folders: the web root and server root. When you type in a domain in your browser, you are accessing the index file of the web root folder on that server. The URLs to any other files (such as images) can be specified relative to that and are thus called relative URLs. When opening a website on your local hard drive using the file protocol, such as when you double click a .html file, you may notice that links don't work as intended. This is because on the file protocol the (/) slash is interpreted as the root directory of your computer, not the folder containing the HTML file you opened (which is known as the present working directory). If you ever see relative URLs such as (../) or (../../), those are accessing the parent folder, or grand parent folder, respectively, of the current working directory. It can take some time to understand this; search the web for more if you are curious.